# The Ethics of
# Trade and Aid

**Think Now**

*Think Now* is a brand new series of stimulating and accessible books examining key contemporary social issues from a philosophical perspective. Written by experts in philosophy, these books offer sophisticated and provocative yet engaging writing on political and cultural themes of genuine concern to the educated reader.

Available now:
*Beyond Animal Rights*, Tony Milligan
*The Ethics of Climate Change*, James Garvey
*The Ethics of Metropolitan Growth*, Robert Kirkman
*Just Warriors, Inc.*, Deane-Peter Baker
*Nanoethics*, Dónal P. O'Mathúna
*Personal Responsibility*, Alexander Brown
*Terrorism*, Nicholas Fotion, Boris Kashnikov and Joanne K. Lekea
*War and Ethics*, Nicholas Fotion

Forthcoming:
*Identity Crisis*, Jeremy Stangroom

Series Editors:
**James Garvey** is Secretary of The Royal Institute of Philosophy and author of *The Twenty Greatest Philosophy Books* (Continuum)

**Jeremy Stangroom** is co-editor, with Julian Baggini, of *The Philosophers' Magazine* and co-author of *Why Truth Matters, What Philosophers Think* and *Great Thinkers A-Z* (all Continuum).

# The Ethics of
# Trade and Aid

## Development,
## Charity or Waste?

Christopher D. Wraight

continuum

**Continuum International Publishing Group**

| | |
|---|---|
| The Tower Building | 80 Maiden Lane |
| 11 York Road | Suite 704 |
| London SE1 7NX | New York NY 10038 |

www.continuumbooks.com

**British Library Cataloguing-in-Publication Data**
A catalogue record for this book is available from the British Library.

ISBN:  HB: 978-1-4411-0951-4
       PB: 978-1-4411-2548-4

**Library of Congress Cataloguing-in-Publication Data**
Wraight, Christopher D.
The ethics of trade and aid : development, charity, or waste? / Christopher D. Wraight.
    p. cm.
Includes bibliographical references (p. ) and index.
ISBN 978-1-4411-0951-4 – ISBN 978-1-4411-2548-4
1. Economic development–Moral and ethical aspects. 2. Economic assistance–Moral and ethical aspects. 3. International trade–Moral and ethical aspects. I. Title.

HD75.W73 2011
174–dc22                                                                    2010033353

Typeset by Newgen Imaging Systems Pvt Ltd, Chennai, India
Printed and bound in Great Britain

# Contents

# Introduction

In recent years, international development has been more topical than ever. The 2005 G8 summit of rich nations was devoted to the issue, and grand promises were made by the world's industrial nations (though it's not entirely clear that they've subsequently lived up to them). Celebrities such as Bono, Bob Geldof and Madonna have organized huge fundraising concerts and visited some of the poorest countries on earth to set up orphanages. Billions of dollars from both public and private sources have been given in the form of grants to poor countries or spent on the infra-structure of the development industry. Huge amounts of time are spent haggling over trade deals designed to free up the move-ment of goods and services. The global aid and trade industry is gigantic and high-profile. Even as the global downturn continues to bite, the pressure on countries and governments to maintain aid spending is high: in the UK, the incoming coalition administra-tion in 2010 committed to maintaining levels of aid spending in the face of a severe domestic fiscal downturn.

All of this is controversial. Trade deals are accused of being too favourable to rich countries' corporations, or too protecting of weak state-owned firms, or not 'fair' in other ways. Aid agencies are suspected of wasting funds, engaging with corrupt regimes, or encouraging a dependency on handouts. Despite the vast amounts of money, time and political capital spent on trying to ensure poor countries catch up with rich ones, it remains unclear what works and what doesn't. Despite years of active efforts by charities and aid agencies, global inequality remains stark.

Because of this topicality and controversy, there's no shortage of books aiming to push a particular point of view on the subject. In what follows, we'll take a look at a couple of them in some detail, such as Jeffrey Sachs' *The End of Poverty* and William Easterly's *The White Man's Burden*. The first of these is a plea for more aid, whereas the second is an argument for less of it. And there are even more strident examples of lobbying from both sides of the debate: the ex-World Bank economist Dambisa Moyo's *Dead Aid: Why Aid Is Not Working and How There Is a Better Way for Africa* pulls no punches in its denunciation of the international development industry, whereas campaigns like Live 8 and Make Poverty History are equally vociferous in their support of more and better aid.

This book aims to be different. I won't argue that aid is, in itself, either a good or a bad thing. If you want to be told what to think, then there are plenty of people who'll be happy to oblige. My own view is that the questions surrounding international development are very complex indeed. I don't think there are any simple answers. After spending six years working on some of the issues (three in London, and three in Africa), my views on what works and what doesn't have changed many times. I've witnessed eminent economists and officials getting it desperately wrong, but have also seen committed individuals performing heroics to prevent almost unimaginable levels of suffering. Many of these people, if pressed, would admit to doubts about the rational basis of their actions, even if what they actually do is worthwhile and motivated by the best of intentions.

What I hope this book will do is show how we can come up with more sophisticated positions on the issue of aid and trade. Some of the loudest voices in the current debate aren't necessarily the ones worth listening to. When a celebrity with a flagging career urges you to open your wallet for a pet project, it's wise to think about what his or her motives are. The same goes for well-paid international officials or the heads of unrepresentative and oppressive governments.

However, there is much to be learned from some of the more sober voices within the debate. There's also knowledge to be gained, I think, from looking at what philosophers have said about the core ideas underpinning ethical action in the world. The scale of global poverty is not something that can be addressed in a purely impersonal way, after all – it's a moral challenge, and one that demands a reasoned, reflective response. The study of philosophical ethics can help us to clarify some of our most fundamental approaches to such issues.

Accordingly, as with the other titles in the *Think Now* series, this book takes the philosophical basis of our actions as seriously as the practical questions of what kinds of things work best on the ground. It's organized into three rough sections: a historical overview of the basis of world poverty; a presentation of some relevant parts of ethical theory; and a survey of the realities of the aid business. My hope is that, by the end of the book, you'll have a better understanding of what the key issues are, and some more resources with which to form your own opinions. I'll conclude with some recommendations on what kinds of intervention I think are likely to succeed, and what we should expect of the aid industry, but these will be relatively modest in ambition. I don't pretend to have any monopoly on what the 'right' approach to take is.

While writing this book, I've been very conscious of the tension inherent in these objectives. Some readers may be impatient with the ethical theory presented here, and will want to know more about the practical aspects of aid and development. Philosophy is a pedantic subject, concerned with making distinctions at a very abstract level – some people find this very frustrating. Other readers, though, will want *more* rigour from the philosophical treatment, and could happily dispense with any discussion of the real world and its messiness. I trust, though, that there will be at least some readers who'll want both, who have a drive to make some kind of practical contribution to poverty reduction, but who are

also interested in more abstract questions of ethics and justification. This book is written for them, with the hope that it will prove
thought-provoking.

## SUMMARY OF THE ARGUMENTS

Let's start with the basics. Social and economic rights are not
divided equally between the rich global 'north' and the poor
'south'. The statistics are depressing: a sixth of the world's population live in extreme poverty. More than a billion people have insufficient money to feed themselves adequately. Around 75 million
children receive no formal education, and 9.7 million babies born
around the world will not live to see their fifth birthdays. All of
this is taking place in a global economy which was until very
recently experiencing one of the most impressive periods of
growth in recorded history.

How did this situation arise? The answer lies in the long view of
economic development. The legacy of the industrial revolution,
together with that of the following period of colonization, lies
heavily on many developing countries. Intervention by the industrialized world in the affairs of more economically backward
places has generally been a recipe for disaster, and some aspects
of the contemporary division of wealth can be directly traced to
this unfortunate history. The post-war system of international
economics has also played a major part in the fortunes of different regions around the world. Some countries, like Thailand, were
chronically poor in the latter half of the twentieth century but are
now regarded as developed nations. Others, like Zambia, were
seen in the 1960s as prime candidates for success, but have since
fallen into extreme poverty. Given the complex history of economic relations, it's not immediately obvious where the blame
lies in every case, nor is it obvious what can be done to improve
the situation. However, the fact that so many people remain so

poor in an era of unprecedented wealth is a problem that demands the attention of all of us.

One reaction to this might be indifference: whatever the causes of poverty, we may feel no moral obligation to help those in poor countries. This could be for two reasons: we feel a generalized selfishness and believe we have no moral obligations towards others, or we feel empathy only towards those culturally like ourselves. With respect to both these positions, I consider arguments from the mainstream of Western philosophy, from Plato to Peter Singer, that attempt to present a rational case for caring about others. I argue that there are good reasons for thinking that we have an obligation to help those in need, and that geographical or cultural distance is a weak objection against action. I also reject a common distinction made between acts and omissions, which might be cited as justification for doing nothing. However, I'll also look at some important qualifications of this position, and conclude that our duty to assist those far poorer than ourselves is legitimately balanced by other kinds of considerations, such as the moral priority of those closest to us and our right to enjoy a flourishing life ourselves.

Having argued that we have some kind of moral obligation to assist those in the developed world, I look at some of the classic philosophical theories of how such an obligation might be discharged. Given we ought to do *something*, how do we decide *what* to do? The classic response is utilitarianism, the idea that our actions ought to be determined by their measurable consequences in creating 'utility'. This is, indeed, the mechanism used by most aid professionals. But utilitarianism has many issues – of particular relevance to international development is the sheer technical difficulty in assessing the actions likely to promote the most utility, or even in settling on what 'utility' is best understood as. In addition, it's unclear whether the crudest forms of utilitarianism adequately take account of important concepts such as rights and duties.

These latter concepts are hardly negligible. To enrich the bare bones of a utilitarian account of ethics, other ideas need to be considered. Two of the most important, I argue, are justice and compassion. The former of these is most influentially treated by John Rawls in *A Theory of Justice*, and I briefly look at what his account might look like, suitably modified for the global situation.

The latter idea, compassion, is hardly ever mentioned in development literature. It is perhaps simply assumed that we ought to be motivated by some sense of empathy or pity, but this is rarely articulated. This is a shame, since philosophy has much to say that can enrich and challenge our common-sense notion of what compassion consists in and how it might properly motivate our actions. Aristotle and Rousseau make much of compassion, and the latter in particular places the idea at the centre of his social and political philosophy. To conclude the part of the book concerned with ethical theory, I argue that, properly understood, it is an essential motivator for our engagement with issues of trade and aid.

Having looked at the scale of the problem and at some of the philosophical tools we might use to address it, I turn to the first key activity of the development industry: giving money and resources to poor countries. I look at the enormous variety of activities in this area, from one-woman-band charitable trusts, to massive international aid agencies. How do these bodies operate? Do they pay attention to the issues we've raise earlier? Are they guilty, as some accuse, of wasting resources and feeding corruption? Or do they provide a vital service, in the absence of which the huge gulf between the developed and developing world would be even wider?

In order to make some sense of the global debate on aid, I look primarily at the views of two influential economists who are firmly on different sides of the fence, Jeffrey Sachs and William Easterly. The former argues that the poor world needs a large injection of capital in order to escape an endemic poverty trap, and that current efforts by the rich world to deliver aid ought to be scaled up rapidly and significantly. Easterly, by contrast, thinks that the so-called 'planner' mentality of the aid industry has been responsible for as many disasters as it's solved, and that the amount of aid ought to be reduced in favour of better, more carefully targeted actions. Both men have their detractors. What is clear, however, is that some form of aid from the rich world to the poor is required to fulfil the demands of compassion and justice. Its success can only be properly judged with reference to a reasonable benchmark, and if we assume that donations of cash from the global north to the south will solve the problem of poverty by itself, then we'll be disappointed. However, aid does have an important role to play in facilitating economic progress in the poorest regions of the world, and if set against other reforms, it constitutes an essential part of the solution.

If aid is only part of the answer, though, what else holds the promise of alleviating poverty? Though the giving of money through grants or loans receives most of the headlines, in terms of scale such actions are dwarfed by the volume of international trade. A fairer trading system holds out the hope of more lasting success.

At present, the chances of achieving that are very uneven. Some countries have traded their way out of poverty in recent years (China and India are two of the most prominent examples and are, according to many pundits, headed for superpower status). Others, particularly in Africa, have fared very badly, and account for a tiny proportion of world trade flows. There are a number of reasons for this, some of them consequences of rich-world policy and behaviour. Under current international trade rules, only certain types of goods are not subject to tariffs and protectionist taxes. These are generally high-value products, of the kind manufactured in rich countries, and are therefore traded relatively freely. By contrast, agricultural goods are subject to high import duties and quotas, imposed by rich countries to protect their farming sectors. These are precisely the products that developing countries would (in theory) be able to export, as in the absence of such barriers their low cost of labour would allow them to undercut producers in developed countries. An equitable system of global commerce would seek to reduce or eliminate these distorting taxes and tariffs, creating the 'level playing field' necessary for genuinely fair trade.

Even if the global trading system were reformed along these lines, though, problems would remain: the uneven distribution of resources and access to transport around the world will still require active intervention to assist those communities least able to tap into the global commercial system. Just as in the case of direct financial aid, dogmatic or monolithic strategies will not work. Any reform of the flows of trade will need to be conducted with compassion and a receptive concern for justice.

The final chapter brings all these threads to a conclusion. I offer some very broad thoughts on how the current aid efforts might be reformed to meet the criticisms of Easterly and his supporters. I end on a cautiously optimistic note: given the enormous numbers of people lifted out of poverty in the final years of the twentieth century, there is nothing inevitable about global inequality on a chronic scale. The application of rational policy-making, motivated by compassion and a concern for justice, holds the promise of a more equal world in the future.

## ACKNOWLEDGEMENTS

I'm extremely grateful to Gulden Bayaz, Ranil Dissanayake, Iain Law, Lindsay Mangham, Debbie Palmer, Rob Rudy, Christopher Warne and Nick Wright for reading earlier drafts of the material and making helpful comments. Any errors that remain are my responsibility. I'm also grateful to Tom Crick at Continuum for his incredible patience in overseeing the delivery of the manuscript. The most thanks are due to my wife Hannah for putting up with the lost evenings at the keyboard and for being unfailingly supportive during the long writing period.

# 1   An Unequal World

In October 2007, the British newspaper *The Guardian* launched a campaign to help a small region in Uganda called Katine. Such campaigns are hardly unusual – every year at Christmas, lots of newspapers launch similar appeals. It's something they're expected to do these days, and if they didn't, there would be outraged letters to the editor.

The Katine project was different from most. At the time of this writing, the programme is still in full swing – it's a three-year scheme, a lifetime in terms of the media (although shorter than many projects run by aid agencies).[1] The idea behind it is ambitious: to bring the problems of a tiny community in the heart of Africa, the poorest continent on Earth, to the attention of the *Guardian*'s generally rich-world readership. As the originator of the scheme, editor Alan Rusbridger, wrote:

> Would it be possible to find a way of dramatising an issue so that it held attention beyond Christmas, even for as long as three years? Of connecting the ideas, goodwill, resources and expert knowledge of 15 million readers around the world and focusing them on one problem? Would it be possible to do all this in a way which avoided the classic trap of creating a temporary oasis in a desert?[2]

Over the last three years, the newspaper has carried regular reports from Katine. It has chronicled the attempts of the project's main implementing organizations – the African Medical and

Research Foundation (AMREF) and Food and Agricultural Research Management – Africa (FARM-Africa) – to bear down on the region's range of problems and has charted how successful the scheme has been at solving them.

The reasons for wanting to help Katine seem obvious enough. In his introductory article, Rusbridger lists the crushing burdens on the area's villagers as they attempt to live their lives. Education levels are extremely low, and the schools are poorly equipped and staffed. Disease, including the devastating plagues of malaria and AIDS, is rampant. There are no health facilities within easy walking distance of the village, and those that do exist farther away are often inadequate to deal with Katine's routine health problems. There's no reliable access to clean water, and the availability of food is dependent on capricious harvests. The threat of war and its associated evils – violence against civilians, rape and theft – looms on the horizon. There's no money to invest, and no reserves of capital to provide a basis for future planning. The inhabitants of the village, exhausted by the grind of everyday life, have their hands full just surviving.

The Katine project aims to improve all this. Supported by money donated by the British banking giant Barclays and readers of the newspaper, the programme directors hope to create an exemplar community in the heart of Uganda. By addressing each of Katine's major problems, they expect to alleviate the worst effects of poverty, demonstrating a better way forward for the region and raising awareness of development concerns in the rich world. In the first of a number of six-monthly reports, they outlined their plans as follows:

- Goal
  - To improve the quality of life of the people of Katine
- Specific Objectives
  - Improved community health
  - Improved access to quality primary education
  - Improved access to safe water, sanitation and hygiene

- ■ Improved income-generating
- ■ Communities empowered to engage in local governance
- Expected Outcomes
  - ■ Increased community awareness, access to and utilization of health services in community and health facilities
  - ■ Improved access to quality primary education for all children and greater community involvement in school governance
  - ■ Increased community access to and utilization of improved water and sanitation facilities
  - ■ Improved hygiene practices in households
  - ■ Improved operations and maintenance of water sources
  - ■ Recovery of livelihoods through diversified and improved sources of income
  - ■ Improved access of rural institutions to both advisory services and markets for their products; increased production and income
  - ■ The community demanding and achieving its rights and services
  - ■ The community's increased capacity to plan and budget for its needs
  - ■ Stronger community capacity for data gathering and utilization.[3]

Anyone familiar with the aid industry will recognize this list of objectives – thousands of such documents are produced every year by similar projects around the world. In this case, the Katine project expects to achieve its goals with £2.6 million from Barclays, in addition to reader donations, all within the three- (or four-) year period. These are certainly laudable aims, and you might expect the sustained commitment of a major UK media organization, backed up by experienced aid agencies and an international banking house, to have generated significant goodwill for the project and attracted praise from the newspaper's readers. However, a quick look at the recent articles about the project doesn't reinforce that expectation.

In an article from April 2010, the *Guardian*'s own reporter wrote about a fairly mundane problem with a single aspect of the development plan – getting concrete sanitation platforms, 'sanplats,' accepted by the residents of the villages. AMREF paid for the materials and training to set up a sanplat distribution business, but things didn't quite work out as intended. The reporter spoke to a man who'd been encouraged to set up trade in the platforms:

> Okodo lamented that – like in Ojom – members of his own community had failed to embrace the idea of buying sanplats. Because of the luke-warm response from the community, the masons had to give up. And yet the materials like cement and sand are still available. He hopes the remaining four pieces will be bought soon so that he can pay the masons their money and interest them in making some more. But he is not very optimistic. "See when AMREF was coming, the people thought everything would be provided for free," Okodo said. "In fact, some of them were accusing us of fraud – that AMREF had given the sanplats for free and we were only trying to extort money from them. Our people here just want free things."[4]

This, too, will be a familiar complaint to anyone acquainted with the aid business: despite the money and time that was spent investing in a sanplat business, the villagers proved unable or unwilling to make use of it. They either couldn't afford the sanitation platforms or didn't want to pay for them. As a result, the self-sustaining scheme set up by AMREF has failed, so far at least, to get off the ground.

The comments from the readers of this article – the people Alan Rusbridger was hoping to enthuse with his project – were, on balance, lukewarm. One reader wrote:

> It seems pretty obvious that AMREF have arrived in Katine with a lot of ideas about what should be done and how it should be done. And some of it isn't working. So the problem lies with the Katine residents instead of the AMREF plans? No. AMREF has misunderstood the

problems and/or chosen the wrong solution. How patronising to suggest that Katine residents believe everything should be given to them
for free. They pay for things they consider to be worth it. Presumably,
even though the sanplats are heavily subsidised, the residents would
rather spend their money on other things. But they're not dumb
enough to reject something given to them for free either. Not only is
the Katine project beginning to look shabby, the *Guardian*'s coverage
is getting pretty drab too.

This type of criticism is also familiar to anyone who's ever had
much to do with the aid industry. The distance between the aspir-
ations expressed in policy documents and the reality of implementing them on the ground can be large. As a result, even
supporters of aid, in principle, can become jaded. Disagreements
over what should be done, how it should be done, when it should
be done (or, indeed, whether it should be done) can make it very
hard to form an opinion on the issue of aid and development.

As a reader of this book, you might be in a similar position to
the *Guardian*'s target market. You might agree with Alan Rusbridger
that the plight of the world's poorest is a scandal which ought to
be addressed by the world's richest. You might wonder how you
could make a contribution to such an effort. Or perhaps, like the
contributor quoted above, you despair of the failure of the rich
West to help the developing world and believe that aid programmes should be scaled back or scrapped. Maybe you think
that Africans are poor because of their own laziness and corruption. Or perhaps they're impoverished because the developed
world conspires to rig the global economic system against them,
and the only solution is a drastic overhaul of the international
trading framework.

We'll look at all those various points of view over the course of
the next few chapters. However, the Katine example is interesting,
as it illustrates some salient points that we'll consider in more
detail as we go along. Being a very public project, it attracts more
attention than many other development initiatives, exposing it

to both pro-aid and anti-aid sentiments. Many readers share Rusbridger's commitment to the idea and believe that their dona- tions will secure a better future for the residents of Katine. Others think that the project is a mistake: either the implementation is flawed or the whole idea of handing out cash for projects in Africa is misguided. Cynically, the Katine episode might be nothing more than a way to sell papers, cashing in on the interest in inter- national development generally exhibited by the newspaper's core readership.

I doubt the latter is true. It's good to be sceptical about aid efforts, but not cynical. I have little doubt that the backers of the project have the best intentions and truly mean to do good. How- ever, I also have doubts about whether spending £2.6 million on a single small area in Africa holds out much promise of changing things for the better in any long-lasting way. Consider the same scenario in the UK. Take a relatively poor region of the country, perhaps an urban conurbation of several million people who are suffering from the effects of the post-industrial economy. Would it be a good idea to plough significant sums of money into one small corner of that city, ignoring the rest of it? If there's a really good, specific reason to do so, then perhaps. Otherwise, we might expect that the good effects of the intervention will be lost amid the general backdrop of deprivation, generate division between those who benefit from the largesse and those who don't, or open up areas of inequality where none previously existed.

It's certainly possible to make your own mind up on Katine, as the data is available to anyone with an internet connection. However, even from the very cursory overview of the project and its reception presented here, a few points might well be evident:

- Getting aid interventions right is difficult. Deciding how to spend a sum like £2.6 million (or £26 million, or more) involves a whole series of contentious choices. The risk of the money being wasted or producing effects that weren't intended is high. It's important that spending is carefully considered, just as it would be if the money were being spent on welfare initiatives in a rich country. When cash is thrown at projects without proper attention to possible outcomes, the situation on the ground can deteriorate rather than improve. As the sanplats example shows, simply providing material resources without considering other factors (the village culture, the wider economy, local politics) can lead to problems.

- Choosing the scope of interventions is also hard. Is it better to concentrate on small-scale projects like Katine, since these are more manageable? Or, would it be better to devote time and effort to regional or continent-wide programmes? This is the rough distinction between working on a 'micro' level (assisting small businesses, local health centres or school clusters) and a 'macro' level (providing support for a country's entire budget or working towards a wholesale reform of the political system).[5] Similar problems of scope emerge in managing rich-country government priorities. Indeed, it is interesting to ask whether we can apply the lessons of managing developed economies (like the UK's) to undeveloped ones (like Uganda's). Perhaps the two cases are totally different, or they may be more similar than we think.

- Who should be delivering aid? Do projects like Katine, where the money is spent by a cluster of small charities, provide the best model for assistance? Or would it be better leaving everything up to the giant multinational organizations, like the United Nations and the World Bank? Do newspaper editors in the UK have the best understanding of Africa's problems, or would it be better to let Africans themselves come up with solutions?

- And what about the Africans? Have they made best use of the aid they've already been given? If not, is there a case to be made for withholding aid money, which could then be spent on deserving causes in other parts of the world? Perhaps the reason communities like Katine are poor is because of some

blameworthy factor in the aid recipients, like corruption or laziness. If so, maybe giving *any* kind of aid is unjustifiable. It might
even encourage a culture of dependency and graft, and if we
really want to help, then perhaps we'd better not give anything
at all.

These factors are a mix of practical considerations (how to spend
money most effectively) and ethical ones (how to act in the right
way). The problems of international trade and aid involve both kinds
of thinking. It's no good having a complete understanding of the
minutiae of development finance if one has no idea *why* it's important to help poor people. Similarly, it's pointless to have good intentions but not educate oneself about what works and what doesn't.

This book will look at both the fundamental ethical questions
thrown up by international aid and the practical ways aid might
be administered. In the next chapter, we look at abstract ideas
of right and wrong, good and bad. Before we delve into that
snake's nest, however, we need to devote some time to the facts.
So far, all we have by way of a picture of the plight of the world's
poorest is the general 'shopping list' of the problems in Katine.
As a first step to looking at the issue, we need a better understanding of the nature and scale of deprivation in the poor
world. In addition, we need some account of how the great differences of wealth between the global rich and poor came
about in the first place. In the rest of this chapter, I'll try to sketch
some answers.

The treatment will be necessarily brief (after all, libraries are
filled with world economic histories and books on colonialism,
development and industrialization), so much important detail will
be missed out. Even here, there are areas of controversy that can't
easily be resolved, such as the legacy of the European empires
and the origins of the industrial revolutions. Nonetheless, there *is*
a general shape to the developmental history of the world that's
possible to trace in its broadest sense, and I'll argue here that
some ways of treating the issue are better than others.

## THE GREAT DIVIDE

In the memorable opening to Joseph Conrad's *Heart of Darkness*, Marlow looks at the River Thames as if seeing it through the eyes of ancient Roman conquerors.

> Imagine the feelings of a commander of a fine – what d'ye call 'em? – trireme in the Mediterranean, ordered suddenly to the north; run overland across the Gauls in a hurry; put in charge of one of these craft the legionaries, – a wonderful lot of handy men they must have been too – used to build, apparently by the hundred, in a month or two, if we may believe what we read. Imagine him here – the very end of the world, a sea the colour of lead, a sky the colour of smoke, a kind of ship about as rigid as a concertina – and going up this river with stores, or orders, or what you like. Sandbanks, marshes, forests, savages, – precious little to eat fit for a civilized man, nothing but Thames water to drink.[6]

'And this also,' says Marlow, 'has been one of the dark places of the earth.' To write such a passage in 1902 – at the apogee of the British Empire – might have struck some readers as an impressive leap of the imagination. To many Victorian Britons, their country's rise to dominate the world must have seemed both inexorable and predestined. The idea that Britain had once seemed as barbarous and primitive to the Roman invaders as the slowly unfurling African continent did to Europeans would have snagged at the pride of a self-confident people, happy in the knowledge of their technical, economic and moral mastery of the globe.

Of course, there had been many times when Britain was a mere backwater in the march of human development. For long periods of the world's history, Conrad's countrymen had been on the fringes of civilization, and any classically educated scholar turned out by a reputable public school would have been well aware of that. And yet, the interesting thing about Conrad's flight of imagination is how inaccurate his comparison is. Though there were important differences between the Romans and the Britons in the first century AD, they were not as profound as those between the

European colonizers of the nineteenth century and the native inhabitants of the countries they conquered during the expansion of their empires. In fact, there has *never* been such a sudden and wide disparity of wealth in the world as the one that emerged then and continues into the present day. The story of a rich, developed world existing alongside an impoverished, developing one is not one that past epochs have known. Instead, it is a product of the last two hundred years. Before then, there had been nothing remotely on the same scale.

When we discuss the current wide disparities of wealth across the globe, we're accustomed to talking as if the existence of chronically poor countries is some kind of aberration: a product of capitalism, perhaps, or of the colonial era. To think in such terms, though, is to get things entirely the wrong way round. For most of human history, virtually everyone was poor. Except for a tiny elite sitting at the top of the pyramid, humans throughout their historical existence have lived on the edge of survival, eking out a perilous existence fraught with food shortages, disease, poverty, vulnerability to natural disasters, lawlessness and ignorance. The reason we don't generally think of history in these terms is partly because we're fortunate enough to live in an age of extraordinary wealth (across large parts of the globe at least), and partly because the stories of the past we read when we study history were written by members of that tiny elite which dominated resources and power.[7] Consider, for example, this description of European life in the mid-seventeenth century:

> The routine of government was ill-organised; politicians worked with inadequate help; honesty, efficiency and loyalty were comparatively rare, and the average statesman seems to have worked on the assumption that a perpetual leakage of funds was inevitable. [. . .] Bloodshed, rape, robbery, torture and famine were less revolting to a people whose ordinary life was encompassed by them in milder forms. [. . .] Discomfort was too natural to provoke comment; winter's cold and summer's heat found European man lamentaby unprepared, his houses too

> draughty and damp for the one, too airless for the other. Prince and
> beggar were alike inured to the stink of decaying offal in the streets, of
> foul drainage about the houses, to the sight of carrion birds picking
> over public refuse dumps or rotting bodies swinging on the gibbets.[8]

It's a description we could apply to some of the modern world's most impoverished trouble spots, such as the Democratic Republic of Congo or Somalia. Today, the country about which this passage was written makes BMWs and solar panels, and does rather well in World Cup finals.

There was of course plenty of economic fluctuation among regions as various civilizations did better or worse at coping with change. There were some very good times to be a peasant in England, and some very bad times too. Until about 1800, though, there would have been a roughly equal number of good times to be a hunter-gatherer in Africa or a farmer in India. The factors that determined how prosperous a region was were fairly constant across the world. Despite the fact that Conrad's Romans were in a position to look down their noses at the ancient Britons when they sailed up the Thames, the gulf between the two groups' living standards was small, and their positions could be reversed quite quickly if circumstances changed. The key constant was that the vast bulk of the population *everywhere* was poor, and subject to the same kinds of threats to livelihood and security that we associate today with the most disadvantaged parts of the world.

So the first question we should ask is not, 'why have some places become so poor?' but 'why did some places get so rich?' What happened to lift some parts of the world out of the squalor that once affected all of it?

## ULTIMATE CAUSES

To answer that question properly, by going back to the very first principles and trying to come up with a properly causal explanation, is a difficult task. In Conrad's time, the chances are the explanation would have been couched in cultural or religious terms. A popular idea was that there were some groups who had a set of attributes best suited for encouraging prosperity and progress. So it was that the social theorist Max Weber could write about the 'Protestant work ethic', that mix of piety, application and self-denial, to explain the burgeoning wealth and power of the northern European countries in the nineteenth century:

> In order that a manner of life so well adapted to the peculiarities of capitalism could be selected at all, i.e. should come to dominate others, it had to originate somewhere, and not in isolated individuals alone, but as a way of life common to whole groups of men. This origin is what really needs explanation. [T]he *greed for gold* of a Neapolitan cab-driver or *barcaiuolo*, and certainly of Asiatic representatives of similar trades, as well as of the craftsmen of southern European or Asiatic countries, is, as anyone can find out for himself, very much more intense, and especially more unscrupulous than that of, say, an Englishman in similar circumstances. The universal reign of absolute unscrupulousness in the pursuit of selfish interests by the making of money has been a specific characteristic of precisely those countries whose citizen-capitalistic development, measured according to Occidental standards, has remained backward.[9]

Weber's emphasis was on the moral characteristics of a particular group as the primary determinant of their economic success. He thinks in terms of nations or religious affiliations having such defining features, and this approach has been very influential. Such an analysis can be taken further and used to explain success by race or genetic type. In his wonderful satire on the typical European attitude towards less-developed parts of the world, *English Passengers*, Matthew Kneale gives us a chilling picture of explanations a Victorian anthropologist might have used to justify or explain his own culture's economic and technological superiority:

> There is, in truth, no finer manifestation of the destiny of men than this mighty institution of imperial conquest. Here we see the stolid and

fearless Saxon Type, his nature revealed as never before as he strides
forth in his great quest, subduing and scattering inferior nations – the
Hindoo, the American Indian, the Aboriginal race of Australia – and
replacing these with his own stalwart sons.[10]

Given the terrible crimes that have been committed in the name
of racial 'superiority' over the last couple of centuries, though, it's
not surprising that such explanations of economic success have
become, to put it mildly, controversial.

More recently, the American academic Jared Diamond has
argued that personal characteristics determined by culture or
race are far less important factors in economic success than environmental ones, like climate, available crops, and types of domes-
ticable animals. In his influential book *Guns, Germs and Steel*, he
introduces dozens of compelling examples in which the kind of
environment a community finds itself in explains the decisions
and strategies they adopt in order to survive. The Eurasian peoples,
he argues, have done well over the last few centuries mostly
due to a happy combination of geographical factors, and not
because they inherently possessed superior qualities of ingenuity
or fortitude:

> The striking differences between the long-term histories of people in
> different continents have been due not to innate differences in the
> people themselves but to differences in their environments. I expect
> that if the populations of Aboriginal Australia and Eurasia could have
> been interchanged during the Late Pleistocene, the original Aboriginal
> Australians would now be the ones occupying most of the Americas
> and Australia, as well as Eurasia, while the original Aboriginal Eurasians
> would be the ones now reduced to downtrodden population
> fragments in Australia.[11]

Diamond has the benefit – unlike Weber – of having access to a
much greater range of scientific data on the ecological histories of
the countries he writes about. He's therefore able to demonstrate the importance of some surprising factors, such as, say, the

extreme difficulty of domesticating zebras. If this doesn't sound like a very pertinent example, consider the parallel of the Eurasian horse. Horses did prove tameable, and were thereafter indispensable in the development of the economies where they were employed, whether as transport, agricultural assistance, cavalry, or even food. Without the horse, the Eurasian economies would have had to find alternative means of providing these things, and in doing so would have depleted their resources in other areas. Parts of the world where the domesticated horse didn't exist were therefore at a significant disadvantage. The equivalents in such places, including zebras, were so hard to control that any attempts to do so were quickly abandoned. As Diamond points out, zebras are still virtually untameable due to a number of biological features – they're almost impossible to lasso, and become impractically dangerous as they age (more zookeepers are injured by zebras than by tigers, apparently).[12]

Taken individually, Diamond's examples may not amount to much. Considered collectively, they present a powerful case for the natural environment being a principal determinant of technological and economic success. Here is a list of some of the most important:

- Availability of local crops suitable for cultivation
- Availability of animals capable of being domesticated, especially big mammals
- Generation of epidemic diseases
- Ease of migration and diffusion between geographical areas
- Terrain type and soil fertility
- Relationship between continental size and population[13]

We'll come across more examples of such ecological factors later in the book, particularly with reference to epidemic diseases.

The debate about the ultimate causes of various nations' success or failure may seem purely academic, but it is important in terms of the discussions to come. If Weber is right, and cultural

factors determine whether a nation succeeds or fails, then we
might feel inclined to *blame* the less prosperous for their lack of
progress (and applaud the richest for being free from such
destructive tendencies). If personal characteristics are the decisive
factor, then the failure of some communities to advance is something we could conceivably hold them to account for. Consider
the parallel with individuals: if someone had ended up poor due
to being greedy, quarrelsome and dishonest, we'd be less likely to
sympathize with them than if they'd been the victim of an external disaster, or had been raised in an environment where they'd
never had a chance to get started.

An attitude of blame is certainly often taken up in current
debates on aid and development. The inhabitants of poor countries are sometimes accused of being 'essentially corrupt', and
hence unwilling to make the best use of things around them. If a
society has historically been poor because its inhabitants are
unscrupulous and conniving, the argument runs, then sending
them money is probably a waste of time. This attitude is extremely
widespread: a survey carried out for the UK Department for International Development (DFID) found that only 21 per cent of
respondents were 'active enthusiasts' of aid. Of those who were
described as 'mainstream interested' (the next level of supportive-
ness down), 40 per cent thought that local corruption made it
pointless to send money abroad. Other groups of respondents
were even more pessimistic.[14]

However, if the real reason a region has historically been poor
is because of factors outside the inhabitants' control, like the
environment, then we'd be much less likely to blame them for
their plight, and may be more willing to assist them. So the difference between a Weber-style account of success and the Diamond
version is more than purely academic – it has a bearing on our
moral response to the situation.

There's no simple answer here, of course, but there's also no
doubt that environmental factors have been extremely important determinants of economic and social progress. It may be

possible to construct some account of how ethnic or genetic predispositions pre-destine certain races to prosperity or penury, but one would have to work very hard to counter Diamond's convincing demonstrations of social progress, and work very carefully to avoid the worst kind of unthinking racism that vitiated so many nineteenth-century theorists. What should be evident is that the rich world enjoys many natural advantages over the poor world. Even if there have been especially gifted individuals or communities which have taken advantage of these particularly well, we should still be cautious about giving the rich world complete credit for its prosperity and blaming the poor world for its deprivation – the real story is far more nuanced and complicated.

If Diamond is right, and it's things like climate and geography that have in large part enabled us in the rich world to prosper, we should feel very much less smug about 'our' success, and much more humble about lecturing the world's poor about their prospects. This is a theme we'll return to later.

## STEAM-POWERED PROGRESS

Whatever the ultimate reasons some places did better then others, it's much less contentious to pick out the key point in history at which near-universal global poverty began to change into the divergent model we see around us today. The key factor was the change that took place in northwest Europe in the eighteenth and nineteenth centuries in the way it produced food and manufacturing goods, a revolution that propelled the region into an era of unparalleled growth and development.

Before then, although technological progress had continued steadily for hundreds of years, European society was still caught in the 'Malthusian trap'. Whenever circumstances conspired to improve the material conditions of the population (a series of good harvests, lack of war, plague, and so on), the birth rate would rise and the death rate would fall. This would lead to rapid population growth and a greater number of mouths to feed. Increased consumption depleted resources and drove conditions back down again. Soon population pressure restored everyone to a state of bare subsistence, since there was at the time no way of radically increasing resource production to keep up with population growth. The only way to restore material conditions was to introduce some major fall in the birth rate or rise in the death rate. So it was, for example, that the conditions of the poorest members of society only improved after catastrophic natural disasters like the Black Death, the pandemic of bubonic plague which decimated Europe's population and freed up more resources per head.

The Malthusian effect gets its name from Thomas Malthus, who wrote famously at the beginning of the nineteenth century of the inevitability of social stagnation. His assumption was that, when resources remain finite, population growth will always be checked when it reaches the limit of what the land can provide. The closer to that limit a population gets, the worse the material living standards will be for the majority.[15]

Malthus, of course, was wrong – at least for the rich world of the twenty-first century. Something changed to enable the cycle to be broken. The key factor was advancements in technology, and when they came, the pace of change was swift and decisive. The effects of just a few innovations clustered together in a small area – the steam engine, chemical fertilizers, iron and steel production – dramatically galvanized the making of almost every kind of product. From the early nineteenth century onward, first in Britain and then across Europe, the manufacture of material goods was harnessed to the extraordinary power of fossil fuels, allowing an explosion in quantity and quality and lifting the Malthusian curse. For the first time in history, living conditions could rise over a long period without creating a concomitant pressure on resource production. The means to escape the necessity of near-universal poverty had been discovered.

This remarkable increase in production brought significant social changes in its wake. The first countries to industrialize, like Britain and Germany, went from being primarily agrarian societies to ones based around cities. The majority of the population moved away from scattered rural settlements to become members of burgeoning conurbations. This in turn had a number of implications. The clustering together of large numbers of people fuelled further technological innovation. The creation of huge urban areas also allowed people to become more specialized in the kinds of functions they performed. Rather than having to live in a subsistence manner as they might have done in their original environment, people were increasingly channelled into a single productive role (working as a miller, or in an ironworks, or in domestic service). They were able to buy food with their wages rather than grow it themselves, and thus could devote even more time to their primary role within the economy. Innovation and specialization helped the industrial economies to become even more efficient.

Following the catalyst of industrialization, European societies entered a virtuous circle of ever-increasing returns. Technological changes continued and brought new wealth, which encouraged further investment, which yielded further wealth, and so on. The very long period of more-or-less static economic activity had been replaced by one where the expectation was for growth. The figures are truly astonishing. The real income of a person in England, having remained static since reliable figures had begun to emerge in the thirteenth century, rose ten-fold between the middle of the nineteenth century and the present day. Plotted on a graph, the sudden jump is precipitous.[16]

Other factors made the outlook for individuals markedly better. Couples began having fewer children, enabling individuals to inherit large shares of the wealth being created. The life prospects of the very richest and the very poorest began to converge. In pre-industrial England, the life expectancy of the rich was greater than that of the poor by almost 20 percent, and the literacy rate was greater by nearly 200 percent. In modern England, the difference in life expectancy is below 10 per cent and the difference in literacy is only 14 per cent.[17] Industrialization not only generated wealth, it also began to make society less unequal.

In modern language, we're accustomed to using the terms 'developed' and 'developing' to describe the richest and poorest countries. We'd perhaps be better off using the terms 'industrialized' and 'non-industrialized', since this captures the key difference between the two economic systems. One system uses technology to escape the constraints of limited food supplies and population pressure, while the other remains trapped in a subsistence framework. In the latter kind of society, people spend all their time trying to find enough food to eat and attending to immediate needs, rather than contributing to a community which has a wide range of goals and being able to make the best use of their skills and potential.

Of course, the effects of the industrial revolution weren't confined to the countries where it originated. Another effect of the technological race was the development of far more potent means of communication, both physical (steam-powered ships and trains) and in terms of information transmission (the telegraph). This enabled news of the fruits of the industrial revolution to travel fast and far. As a result, the profound transformations experienced by nineteenth-century European society were soon felt across the globe. For better or worse, the era of colonialism, in which the newly dominant nations of Europe flexed their steam-powered muscles across the entire planet, had begun. Disappointingly, though, the spread of industrial knowledge did not bring a universal rise in living standards. Europe got richer, and much of the rest of the world got poorer. To see why that happened, we need to look at the means by which the industrial revolution was exported.

## IMPERIAL RIGHTS AND COLONIAL WRONGS

Colonialism has received bad press for a long time. During the latter half of the twentieth century, it seemed obvious to most people that the period of European domination, in which most of Africa, Southeast Asia, the Middle East and South America were economically or politically subjugated by a handful of countries thousands of miles away, was disastrous in both moral and practical terms. An academic discipline, 'post-colonialism', has been launched to chart the ways in which colonized peoples were held back by the colonizers.

There are, however, some who dissent from this negative view. The historian Niall Ferguson has written an influential defence of the British Empire, the most successful of the European imperial projects in terms of geographical coverage. Though Ferguson acknowledges the many problems brought about by the British colonizers, he thinks that, on balance, the Empire was a beneficial phenomenon:

> Of course no one would claim that the record of the British Empire was unblemished. [. . .] Yet the nineteenth century Empire undeniably pioneered free trade, free capital movements and, with the abolition of slavery, free labour. It invested immense sums in developing a global network of modern communications. It spread and enforced the rule of law over vast areas. Though it fought many small wars, the Empire maintained a global peace unmatched before or since.[18]

So who's right? Did the colonial period give the unindustrialized world its best shot at catching up with the industrialized nations? Or did it widen the gap between the haves and have-nots?

The first thing to note is the sheer scale of the technological and economic superiority of the Europeans compared with the rest of the world. As we remarked earlier when discussing Conrad's imaginative journey, though there had been empires and subjugated peoples before, there had never been quite such a gulf between the invaders and invaded. Even before the major period of industrialization, European technology was often far superior to that of native peoples. Diamond recounts the astonishing story of Pizarro's tiny force of Spanish adventurers routing an Inca army numbering perhaps 80,000.[19]

Industrial-era European armies were even more devastating, being able to bring to bear against their enemies terrifying mechanical killing machines that made killing as efficient a process as steelmaking or textile production:

> Operated by a crew of four, the 0.45 inch Maxim could fire 500 rounds a minute, fifty times faster than the fastest rifle available. A force equipped with just five of these lethal weapons could literally sweep a battlefield clear. The battle of Shangani River in 1893 was the first ever use of the Maxim in battle. [. . .] Around 1,500 Matebele warriors were wiped out. Just four of the 700 invaders died. *The Times* reported smugly that the Matebele 'put our victory down to witchcraft, allowing that the Maxim was a pure work of an evil spirit.'[20]

The psychological shock to invaded native populations who were faced with such overwhelming technological superiority must have been tremendous. Entire systems of belief, predicated on certain assumptions about the world and how it operated, would have been swept away in a brutally short period of time.

Military or psychological damage, though, was not always the most destructive aspect of the colonial invasions. European diseases caused absolute devastation among populations that had no hereditary resistance to them. Smallpox, measles, influenza and other contagions were responsible for millions of deaths during the first phases of European expansion. In 1492, the native population of Hispaniola was about eight million. By 1535, little more than fifty years after the arrival of the first Europeans, there were none left at all.[21]

It's true that some of the major theatres of European expansion, like Africa and tropical Asia, had virulent diseases of their own, such as malaria and cholera, which killed thousands of European settlers and slowed down the expansion into such places for a while. However, even in the most unpromising situations, the power of European technology was able, eventually, to tame the land sufficiently to allow permanent settlement and exploitation. The cost of doing so was frequently born by the natives, though, and there were horrific examples of exploitation. The most infamous is the Belgian Congo, where a tiny European 'nation', founded only in 1830, managed to brutalize a region larger than England, France, Germany, Spain and Italy combined. The Belgians' desire to develop a rubber industry led to widespread atrocities, all apparently sanctioned or ignored by the colonial authorities:

> As the rubber terror spread throughout the rainforest, it branded people with memories that remained raw for the rest of their lives. [. . .] With "humanitarian" ground rules that included cutting off hands and heads, sadists like [colonial administrator] Fiévez had a field day. The station chief at M'Bima used his revolver to shoot holes in Africans' ear lobes. Raoul de Premorel, an agent working along the Kasai river, enjoyed giving large doses of castor oil to people he considered malingerers. When villagers, in a desperate attempt to meet the weight quota, turned in rubber mixed with dirt or pebbles to the agent Albéric Detiège, he made them eat it.[22]

Adam Hochschild, in his memorable book *King Leopold's Ghost*, reckons that such barbarism on the part of the colonial forces reduced the native population by half, or about ten million people.[23] This was an extreme example – not all colonial administrations were as appalling as that of Belgium. None, however, were imposed with the informed consent of the native population, and all required the use of force to maintain control.

So far, then, the impact of colonial expeditions looks pretty bleak. But what about the positive face of the expansion of the industrial nations: the roads, schools, health care, and so on? The temptation of some critics of colonialism has been to ignore the substantial investment in infrastructure undertaken by Europeans in places like India and Africa, a tendency that was memorably satirized by Monty Python in 'The People's Front of

Judea', from their film *Monty Python's Life of Brian*: 'But apart from better sanitation and medicine and education and irrigation and public health and roads and a freshwater system and baths and public order . . . what have the Romans done for us?' Surely, the colonial authorities performed similar feats of administration and deserve some credit for it?

In fact, there were huge transfers of capital and expertise from the colonizer countries to the colonized. When travelling in rural areas of Africa today, it's impossible not to be struck by the remnants of the pre-war era, such as disused railway lines and crumbling trading posts. In such circumstances, it seems as if the colonial period was just about the only time that any significant investment was being made in the economic fabric of the continent. In support of this viewpoint, Niall Ferguson makes an interesting comparison between the investment flows of the British Empire, especially compared to those of the modern United States:

> Investment in domestic industry would have been better for Britain than investment in far-flung colonies, while the cost of defending the Empire was a burden on taxpayers. [. . .] One historian, writing in the new *Oxford History of the British Empire*, has gone so far as to speculate that if Britain had got rid of the Empire in the mid 1840s she could have reaped a "decolonisation dividend" in the form of a 25 per cent tax cut. [. . .] British imperial power relied on the massive export of capital and people. But since 1972 the American economy has been a net *im*porter of capital.[24]

The point of the comparison is that British imperial investment was so profound that, on some readings, it actually acted against the country's best interests. The benefits of the free movement of capital accrued most enduringly to the overseas territories of the Empire, who also benefited from the rule of law and the imposition of stable institutions.

Opponents of colonialism, of course, argue that such investments were made with the sole intention of extracting mineral wealth from the interior of colonies and getting it to Europe as quickly as possible. Though there are many examples of this (just look at the way railways in Africa connect mines to ports, rather than cities to cities), it's too simple an explanation for the total commitment of resources in conquered territories. Many Europeans had a genuinely liberal and enlightened outlook towards the indigenous peoples they came to rule over. The motives of the adventurers, missionaries, chancers and settlers who left the industrial world to forge a livelihood in Africa or India were mixed: some good, some naive, some bad. The famous explorer David Livingstone summarized his intentions in promoting missionary work in Africa in his published diaries:

> This account is written in the earnest hope that it may contribute to that information which will yet cause the great and fertile continent of Africa to be no longer kept wantonly sealed, but made available as the scene of European enterprise, and will enable its people to take a place among the nations of the earth, thus securing the happiness and prosperity of tribes now sunk in barbarism or debased by slavery; and, above all, I cherish the hope that it may lead to the introduction of the blessings of the Gospel.[25]

Here we find a statement of the complete range of European motivations: the promotion of European enterprise, the elimination of slavery, the establishment of prosperity for the native peoples, and the propagation of the Gospel. Livingstone's legacy is much debated, but it seems clear enough from this passage, and from others in the book, that he was sincere in his desire to do good for Africa. Indeed, in countries where his anti-slavery activities were concentrated, like Malawi, he is still remembered with respect and affection.

Even when the colonialists' intentions were good, though, they had a decidedly mixed record in improving the economic potential of the regions they settled in. Though some trailblazers, like Cecil Rhodes, made their fortunes, others found it cripplingly hard to extract a living from the harsh soils of Africa and India. In some places, European methods of agriculture proved much less effective than the traditional methods of the native inhabitants, with ruinous effects on the health of the soil and long-term agricultural prospects.[26] Livingstone's vision of an African paradise, freed from barbarism through the enlightened guidance of the white man, proved frustratingly difficult to achieve. As the early settlers were to discover, often to their heavy cost, sometimes a region's failure to become economically fruitful wasn't down to the indolence or backwardness of the natives, but instead was the result of environmental factors similar to those listed by Diamond. Turning malaria-infested swamps into rolling farmland was difficult, even for Europeans armed with the most remarkable technology.

So the colonial period, taken as a whole, throws up a whole range of contradictions. For every sadistic administrator in the Congo, there was an idealistic missionary in Malawi; for every competent industrialist investing in enduring infrastructure and institutions, there was an incompetent ingénue trampling over long-established patterns of cultivation. From such wildly varying motives and outcomes, we might conclude that it's impossible to come to a balanced assessment of colonialism's impact. Despite the complications, though, we can make some judgements. While some good things were done under its name, I think we should regard colonialism as a great and terrible mistake for two reasons.

The first is one of simple morality. Suppose that Ferguson were right, and the practical benefits of the colonial era outweighed the costs to the conquered natives. If we were somehow able to compare the reality of today with a hypothetical state where colonialism never took place, we might discover that Africa (and other colonised regions of the world) are better off now in economic terms than they would have been had the Europeans never arrived. Does this make the seizure of other peoples' lands right? Does it somehow expunge the appalling loss of life inflicted by the Maxim guns? I don't see that it does. The aboriginal inhabitants of Africa or other places had *rights* to their land – it was their home, and their claims to it trumped any pragmatic benefit to them that might have been gained by the Europeans' taking it from them without consent.

Of course, it would be wrong to assume that there was no war, slavery or deprivation in the pre-industrial parts of the world before the white man came on the scene. Plenty of indigenous communities had their lands appropriated after battles with other indigenous groups, and the idea that pre-colonial Africa and South Asia were utopias of peace and plenty is entirely misleading. Nonetheless, this does not excuse the actions of the Europeans who trampled across land rights with such impunity and on such an enormous scale. It cannot even be argued that the colonialists were ignorant of native demands for self-determination: they regarded themselves as enlightened, liberal agents of civilization, steeped in the traditions of Mill and Locke. At the very least, the waiving of rights over lands which were near sacred in developed parts of the world in the name of economic progress and social improvement was arrogant and naive; at worst, it was breathtakingly hypocritical.

Second, it seems to me that, even in practical terms, the utterly ruinous cost to the world's poor of colonial-era mistakes and indifference cannot be redeemed by its relatively few successes. Though drawing up a comprehensive assessment of the colonial enterprise is difficult, it is not impossible. Jeffrey Sachs and William Easterly, two writers on aid with very different views on how it ought to be delivered, agree that the imperialist project was a disaster for the countries it subsumed. As Sachs says:

> Far from lifting Africa economically, the colonial era left Africa bereft of educated citizens and leaders, basic infrastructure, and public health facilities. The borders of the newly independent states followed the arbitrary lines of former empires, dividing ethnic groups, ecosystems, watersheds, and resource deposits.[27]

Easterly devotes plenty of space to the colonial project in his critique of international aid, *The White Man's Burden*, and ends up
being scarcely less damning. He acknowledges that there were
long periods of well-intentioned administration, and even some
successes on the ground:

> European medicine made a lot of progress against smallpox and sleep-
> ing sickness in the first half of the twentieth century. Colonial mater-
> nity clinics also contributed to a fall in infant mortality. The end result
> was that death rates fell and population rose in the twentieth century
> in colonial Africa.[28]

Despite these limited gains (Easterly also mentions improvements, such as the expansion of railway networks, other public
health gains and the increase in irrigated land), actual growth
rates in the colonies were unimpressive:

> Under the theory that "whites know best", colonialists forced devel-
> opment schemes on the locals rather than respecting their eco-
> nomic choices. [. . .] African growth under the imperialists was modest:
> 0.6 percent per annum from 1870 to 1913 and the 0.9 percent per
> annum from 1913 to 1950. [. . .] It is hard to see any positive overall
> effect of colonial rule compared to independent states.[29]

Given that there was so little practical gain from the colonial
period, the injustice of the occupation of so many lands can hardly
be justified. Though there are bright points amid the darkness,
the balance of charges comes down firmly in the negative.
European intervention across the rest of the world inflicted terrible wrongs and delivered little in the way of positive development. It failed to transfer the industrial processes that had worked
in Europe to non-industrialized regions. Even when well-
intentioned, the lack of respect paid to native rights and property,
combined with an occasionally frightening level of incompetence,
meant that rich-world interventions in the most underdeveloped

countries contributed to, rather than narrowed, the widening gulf of prosperity between them.

## THE POST-COLONIAL WORLD

The colonial period came to an end at the beginning of the twentieth century, destroyed by two world wars and a global economic depression. The technological progress of the industrial era didn't end, and the developed world continued to see a gradual, albeit fractious, upward trend in living standards. With a few exceptions, however, the colonized parts of the world – chiefly Africa, India and Southeast Asia, failed to benefit from economic growth.

In the aftermath of the First World War and the dissolution of the old empires, the world divided into three ideological camps. The 'First World' was the name given to the group of countries who retained relatively open market economies, led by the democracies of Western Europe and the United States. Though years of war had stripped them of their overseas possessions, they retained enough economic vigour to maintain a gradual improvement in domestic living standards. After the end of the Second World War, the First World countries, led by the United States as the world's industrial powerhouse, enjoyed a period of sustained growth, as well as considerable social liberation.

In contrast, the 'Second World' – those countries that had adopted a communist economy – had a much rockier ride. By isolating their markets from the wider world and adopting totalitarian governments, they failed to take advantage of either wealth creation or social freedom. Crippled by corruption, repression and inefficiency, the Second World almost completely dissolved towards the end of the last century. Most of its former members transferred, rather imperfectly, to the First World model of economic management. Some, such as the eastern European countries that had traditionally been a part of the cultural West, did very well. Others, such as Russia and Belarus, charted a more precarious route. Yet, despite their difficulties, most former Second World countries are not now among the world's poorest and retain high levels of industrialization.

The Third World, largely comprising countries that had been colonized by Europeans, was different. Third World governments generally avoided going down the trails blazed by the First and Second. They tended to keep their economies closed (at least by the standards of, say, Britain and America), but also avoided the most repressive forms of communist rule. They represented a 'third way' in a sense that's become familiar to anyone who lived through the Blair years in the UK: a compromise between the extremes of socialism and capitalism. From the rush of independence in the 1950s and 1960s until the fall of the Second World, Third World countries searched for a distinctive way to manage their economies. In doing so they rejected both the lessons of colonialism (to the frustration of the West) and, largely, the lessons of Marx (to the annoyance of the East).

Sadly, the results were terrible. In 1955, the GDP of Zambia was seven times less than that of the UK.[30] At the turn of the millennium, the UK's GDP was roughly twenty-eight times bigger.[31] Half a century of self-rule had plunged Zambians into worse poverty than they had known under colonial administration, even as their former imperial masters continued to improve their own material prospects. As a result, the term 'Third World' rapidly became a byword for poverty and destitution. The hopes of sufficiency and economic independence that had burned so bright after the withdrawal of the European empires had turned, in a very short time, into the dreadful nightmare we see around us today.

So why did things continue to go so badly wrong for the Third World? Despite the problems we discussed above, some blame the premature withdrawal of colonial government, and advocate a return to the paternalism of the past.[32] It's easy to see why influential policymakers might feel like this. The closing years of the twentieth century saw a number of states in the Third World fail entirely (e.g. Sierra Leone, Liberia and Somalia), which prompted First World intervention in varying degrees. In a world that's interconnected to an even greater degree than that of the Victorians, it's impossible to insulate the rich world from the travails of the poor. Since we can't *ignore* failed states, runs the argument, and since they cannot look after themselves, then perhaps the best thing to do is return to a policy of benign imperialism.

We'll consider aspects of this idea in more detail later, especially with regard to the charge that modern-day aid efforts are imperialism by another name. For the time being, we should remember that the parlous state of many ex-colonized countries is at least partly due to mistakes made by their European administrators. To return to a similar scenario in order to fix those mistakes looks very much like prescribing more of the medicine that caused the problem. Moreover, there's a powerful case to be made that the institutional weakness of many Third World countries stems directly from the post-colonial interventions of the First and Second Worlds – *after* the colonies had gained their nominal independence.

Consider the world situation in the second half of the twentieth century. The First and Second Worlds, which together accounted for the vast share of the planet's power and resources, were locked in a bitter ideological battle. The Third World, while it offered little in the way of reciprocal power, was a vital element in the unfolding game. Africa and Southeast Asia were home to huge reserves of extractable resources. In addition, the propaganda victory of having countries fall in behind one political system or the other was huge. As a result, the major military powers were extremely active in the internal politics of countries whose self-determination had, in theory, been granted.

Once again, the most outrageous example is the Belgian Congo. Having been bled dry by its rapacious European administrators, the colony was granted independence in 1960. Unsurprisingly, many in the new African political class wanted nothing to do with the economic system that had brutalized their country for so long.

One such figure was Patrice Lumumba, the prime minister elected one month prior to independence. His outspoken denunciations of the West were to lead, within a year, to his death.

> Lumumba believed that political independence was not enough to free Africa from its colonial past; the continent must also cease to be an economic colony of Europe. His speeches set off immediate alarm signals in Western capitals. Belgian, British, and American corporations by now had vast investments in the Congo, which was rich in copper, cobalt, diamonds, gold, tin, manganese, and zinc. [. . .] Alternatives for "the problem" were considered, among them poison [. . .], a high-powered rifle and freelance hit men. But it proved hard enough to get close to Lumumba to use these, so, instead, the CIA supported anti-Lumumba elements within the factionalised Congo government, confident that they would do the job. They did. After being arrested and suffering a series of beatings, the prime minister was secretly shot in Elizabethville in January 1961.[33]

After Lumumba, Congo (afterwards Zaire) was ruled by Mobutu Sese Seko, a tyrant and a thug who drained the remaining resources of the country even more efficiently than his predecessors. In return for millions of dollars of aid money (most of which was stolen), the heart of Africa remained solidly pro-Western, and the majority of its people continued to suffer under the corrupt and dictatorial government. An opportunity had been missed, and the results, tragically, are still with us today.

The Lumumba assassination has become infamous, and not all post-colonial interventions (which were committed by both West and East) were as blatant and ruinous. Nonetheless, the idea that the Third World needs *more* political intervention by the developed world generates a slightly hollow ring when placed beside this long and ignoble history of meddling and manipulation.

In addition, it's worth remembering that the global system of economic governance is a creation of the First World powers and has until recent times had very little input from the poorest countries. We'll look at this structure in more detail in Chapter 5 when we consider the ways in which trade imbalances impact poverty, but in order to conclude our historical overview of the world economic situation we need to look briefly at how trade and capital flows are regulated, and what effect this has had on the world's poorest.

## THE RULES OF THE GAME

In the era of the European empires, money and labour flowed freely across large parts of the world. The primacy of European currencies, like the British pound sterling, made it almost as easy for a company to invest in Bangalore as in Britain. Because there were few artificial impediments to the operation of a global market – such as currency controls within trading areas – it was possible for money to 'follow' opportunity in an efficient manner. We're familiar today with the terms 'globalization' or the 'global village' used to capture a similar state of affairs, but it was really during the imperial era that such ideas first gained purchase.

It took the collapse of the European empires and the ruinous cost of two world wars for the first age of globalization to come to a close. Between the wars, restrictions on trade drastically reduced the flow of goods and capital around the world. Rich and poor countries alike became more 'protectionist' by restricting imports and maintaining high prices for national producers. As a result, the vigour of global trade diminished. The 1930s, blighted as they were by the Great Depression, saw a precipitous (though temporary) reversal in the economic fortunes of the world's rich countries.

In the post-war years, the apparent weaknesses of the protectionist tendency gave rise to a new economic consensus. In July 1944, while the last dramas of the conflict were still being played out, the Allied nations signed up to a series of agreements designed to ensure greater international economic stability. The conference where the agreements were hammered out was the United Nations Monetary and Financial Conference, and the venue was the Mount Washington Hotel in Bretton Woods, New Hampshire. Delegates such as the British economist John Maynard Keynes participated in a global network of agreements intended to prevent the fragmentation of the world's trading zones and a restoration of a flat(ish) pitch for international competition. Currencies were first pegged to the dollar, then became fully convertible. Agreements were drawn up in the subsequent decades to reduce the tariffs on goods crossing borders in order to accelerate the growth of trade. As a result of the liberalization of international trade, global wealth grew sharply, and the economies of the participant countries gradually recovered from lows of the inter-war years.

This system, suitably modified as the years have passed, is the one that currently obtains. The institutions that govern it are sometimes called the 'Bretton Woods' institutions, after the hotel that hosted the initial conference. A simplified list of these and other important bodies in the world system is:

- The International Monetary Fund (IMF). Most countries in the world now belong to the IMF, although its origins and leadership come from the First World nations. Among other functions, it uses money taken from a central pool to assist countries suffering from short-term economic problems (such as being unable to pay their bills). Although all member countries contribute to the central pool, not all members contribute the same amounts, nor do they all have the same influence over the Fund's policy. When the IMF intervenes to assist a country, it may attach certain conditions to its loans. Some of these, such as the 'Structural Adjustment' programmes, have become controversial.
- The World Bank. This is actually a group of five agencies, but the term 'World Bank' is often used to refer to the functions of just one of them: the International Bank for Reconstruction and Development (IBRD). The principal function of the World

Bank is to provide low-cost loans to poor countries to assist them with long-term economic development. Traditionally, this has taken the form of investment in major infrastructure programmes. Like the IMF, the World Bank may impose conditions on disbursements of aid, and these, too, have proved controversial.

- The G8 and World Trade Organization (WTO). Aside from the two financial organizations of the world trading system, there are also bodies charged with drawing up the rules of trade. In the wake of the Bretton Woods conference, the world's richest countries formed the General Agreement on Tariffs and Trade (GATT) to reduce the impediments to the flow of capital and goods around the world. As the global economy liberalized, it was replaced with the WTO, which is currently the 'policeman' for the international trading system. Members of the WTO are expected to abide by the trade rules and can expect sanctions or punitive tariffs if they fail to comply. Trade agreements are still hammered out by the most influential countries operating in the global marketplace. In recent years, these have been the 'G8': Britain, Canada, France, Germany, Italy, Japan, Russia and the United States. The rise of countries such as India, China and Brazil has put pressure on this group to widen.

When protestors talk about reforming the world economic system, they usually mean reforming the IMF, the World Bank, the WTO and the meetings of rich country governments like the G8. They are right to focus on these institutions, since they are the most important international instruments. Together, they have the resources to intervene in poor countries' economies, and the clout to change or enforce the rules of international trade.

So, since the end of the Cold War and the lessening of ideological differences between the world's great powers, how successful has this system been in improving the lot of the world's poorest? The answer is mixed. Some parts of the world, such as the Asian Pacific Rim, have achieved exponential levels of growth. China and India have forged ahead, and are widely tipped to be the economic superpowers of the future. They are two of the winners in the global economic system, and show what can be achieved when economies open up and take advantage of a highly connected world.

On the other hand, some parts of the world, especially sub-Saharan Africa (all those African countries south of the Sahara desert), have fared extremely badly. In 1965, average life expectancy in India was about 48 years, against about 42 years in Africa. Today, average life expectancy in India is 63 years, whereas poor Africans are stuck at 46 years. The difference between Africa and China is even more striking.[34] In effect, the tragedy of endemic poverty has gone from being something that affected almost everyone in the world, to something that affected non-European countries, to something that primarily affects Africa. Of course, there are still regions of abject deprivation in South Asia and elsewhere, but the only continent in the world where economic trends have been relentlessly downward is Africa. The Commission for Africa report, written in 2005, lists the challenges facing the continent:

> Poverty and hunger are deepening in sub-Saharan Africa. The number of poor people is expected to rise from 315 million in 1999 to 404 million people by 2015. Some 34 per cent of the population is undernourished – almost double the figure for the rest of the developing world. The impact of hunger upon the health of Africa's children is hard to measure. Hunger kills more than all the continent's infectious diseases – HIV and AIDS, malaria and tuberculosis (TB) – put together. Early childhood malnutrition has irreversible long-term consequences, not just in health but also in educational achievements and future earning capacity. Other indicators are equally depressing, [and] Africa is the only continent where the proportion of the population in poverty is growing.[35]

It's a grim litany of failure, and one which famously provoked the *Economist* magazine to label Africa 'the hopeless continent' in a 2001 editorial.

It's this scenario that forms the backdrop to the rest of this book. When we talk about the challenges of global poverty, Africa and its problem dominate the discussion. As a result of a combination of environmental factors, the shock of colonialism, the interference of Western powers during the Cold War, and an inability to thrive in the world of the Bretton Woods institutions, Africa has remained stuck in the Malthusian trap even as the rest of the world accelerates away from it. Paul Collier has referred to this predicament as the plight of the 'bottom billion':

> The Third World has shrunk. For forty years the development challenge has been a rich world of one billion people facing a poor world of five billion people. [. . .] This way of conceptualising development has become outdated. For of the five billion, about 80 percent live in countries that are indeed developing, often at amazing speed. The real challenge is that there is a group of countries at the bottom that are falling behind, and often falling apart.[36]

Such is the legacy of recent world economic history. There have been amazing successes, but there is also a lingering and stubborn element of failure. Some African countries have not only failed to prosper from the global boom years of the last couple of decades, but have actually gone backwards.

The contemporary economic situation, then, offers grounds for both despair and hope. On the one hand, it's almost impossible not to be despondent about the prospects for African people trapped in poverty. As we've seen, there has never really been a time when Africa has enjoyed widespread prosperity. On the other hand, the post-war years have shown that regions of the world with similar colonial and Cold War past can break the Malthusian cycle and lift millions out of deprivation. For this reason, current debates about aid and development oscillate wildly between optimism and pessimism. Optimists look at the rapid growth of

China and India and see the chance of ending all global poverty in a relatively short space of time: Jeffrey Sachs' book is called *The End of Poverty: How We Can Make it Happen in Our Lifetime*. Pessimists look at the daunting structural challenges posed by the African situation, some of which we've chronicled here, and see little chance of breaking the cycle. They doubt that the current economic system, and the agencies that run it, are capable of helping Africans out of endemic poverty. As a result, some would rather the money and time spent trying to help Africa were channelled elsewhere, into projects that have a better chance of doing good.

## A MORAL PROBLEM

This brings us back to where we started, to the debate over interventions like the Katine project. We're still not in a position to assess this properly, but we at least can place the issue into some kind of context. In particular, the arguments I've made in this chapter are as follows:

- Long-term historical differences between nations are in large part down to environmental factors, rather than cultural or racial ones.
- Europe's circumstances enabled the industrial revolution to take place, transforming the material conditions for its population.
- The colonial period did not succeed in disseminating this success; in fact, it was a disaster that had terrible consequences for most colonized countries.
- The post-colonial international system has enabled some parts of the world to catch up (notably Southeast Asia), but some other parts (sub-Saharan Africa) have not benefitted.
- As a result, the world's economic 'winners' have never had it so good, nor have there ever been as many of them. But the

difference between them and the world's 'losers' has never been wider. The scale of global inequality is unparalleled in history, and is a moral challenge to us all.

What should be done about this? We'll look at the practical challenges in Chapters 4 and 5. Before that, however, we'll take a step back from pragmatic issues and spend some time talking about ethics in its broadest sense. Since the problem of world poverty is essentially a *moral* problem, it will be helpful to look at what the tradition of Western philosophy has to say about moral decision making, and about what kinds of approaches hold the best prospect of guiding our actions in the right direction.

# 2   The Ethical Imperative

In the previous chapter, we looked at some of the stark realities of the current world economic system and some of the reasons things turned out the way they did. For many people in the developed world, the presence of such obvious disparities in wealth between the richest and poorest countries is a strong motivation to do something about the situation. This might take the form of direct action – leaving behind a well-heeled existence in Europe or North America to work in Africa, for example – or it might involve working in London or Washington DC to bring about change in the global system of political and economic governance. It might prompt an individual to change his or her behaviour in a small way – say, by making a regular donation to charity – or to do something on a larger scale, such as pursue a radically different way of living and working. As someone who bought or borrowed this book, you're most likely concerned about these issues. It may be that, having looked more deeply at the scale of the problem, you're eager to enter the discussion about how aid can be used most effectively. Before we get into that, however, we need to consider another type of person.

This book, as I warned in the introduction, is a study of the application of *philosophical* ideas to current issues of global aid and development. Philosophers are an odd breed. They like to take problems back to their first principles, to look into the core concepts we employ and see whether they stand up to scrutiny. To a philosopher, it might not be at all obvious that the natural response to such manifest inequality is to feel compassion and have a desire to help. Perhaps the best thing to do in such a situation would be to ignore the problem. Or, maybe it isn't a problem at all – it might be best to get on with our own lives, rather than worrying about things that don't concern us.[1]

This attitude may strike you as callous: surely, it's *obvious* that deprivation on such a scale demands some kind of moral response. However, many things that once seemed obvious (like witches having power to curdle the milk and the sun revolving around the earth) no longer do so to most people, in part, because rational individuals took the time to scrutinize them and found them wanting. Modern academic philosophers devote a lot of effort to unpicking our instinctive moral intuitions to see whether they stand up to rational scrutiny. The hope is that, once we've got a clearer picture of the *basis* of our beliefs, we can be more confident about our actual moral behaviour in the real world. We might even change our minds about a few things.

So the rest of this chapter is a look at what mainstream Western philosophy has to say about our ethical choices. We'll look at whether it's rational to be a moral person, whether it's justifiable to care more about those closest to you than those far away, what the difference is between acting and refraining from acting and what that means for an ethical theory of aid and development. In what follows, there will be some abstract ideas, some of which may seem very remote from the concrete business of development policy. However, these ideas have been extremely influential, overtly or covertly, in shaping our general world view over the years. By understanding something about them, we can understand more about the choices people in the development industry have made in the past and continue to make today.

## BEING RATIONAL AND BEING MORAL

One of things that philosophers care deeply about is rationality. At its simplest level, this is the idea that we ought to have good reasons for believing the things we believe. It's no good to say, in response to a query about your convictions, that 'it's just the way things *are*', even if you really think that. To satisfy a philosophical enquiry, you need to look a little deeper into *why* things are the way they are.

What counts as a good reason for doing something is, ultimately, a matter of much debate. There are as many problems with the notion of rationality as there are with everything else in philosophy. There's no real agreement over how reasons give weight to conclusions or whether moral reasoning is the same as reasoning over matters of fact. Yet, despite these difficulties, we can make a few basic points which will have a bearing on what's to come. I suggest that there are three basic ways of assessing a moral argument, and that all three tests need to be passed for that argument to be persuasive.

The first criterion is *factual accuracy*. Beginning with David Hume in the eighteenth century, philosophers have made a sharp distinction between statements of fact and statements expressing moral obligation. In the jargon, they claim that you can't derive an 'ought' from an 'is': knowing that the world *is* a certain way doesn't allow us to infer that we *ought* to behave in a certain way.[2] However reasonable-seeming it is, this position needs to be treated with care. It might lead us to think that moral views are somehow completely divorced from the real world and that we don't need to pay attention to facts to have credible opinions. This would be a mistake. Even though there may be no mechanical way to generate an 'ought' statement from an 'is' statement, being informed about the factual context of an ethical discussion is essential if our judgements are to be taken seriously.

For example, suppose someone thinks that giving aid to Africa is wrong. When pressed to give a reason for her view, she says that 90 per cent of the money spent by aid agencies goes to the salaries for rich consultants, and only 10 per cent goes to the needy poor. Since she thinks this is wrong, she thinks giving aid is wrong too. If her figures are correct, then she might have a good reason for not wanting to donate money to Africa. However, if I were able to show her that she had misread the situation, and that actually only 10 per cent of the donated money went to salaries and expenses, and that the rest went where it was intended to go, then her reason would lose most of its force. The factual argument she was using to arrive at her moral position would be undermined, and she would need to reconsider.

In practice, a lot of disagreements about aid and development are rooted in disagreements over facts. People argue about whether donations of money in fact lead to more corruption, or whether changing the trade rules will in fact lead to wealth creation in poor countries. This can make the business of argument very challenging, since the facts of development economics (as well as those of history, culture and politics) are often highly contentious. At the very least, though, if we're going to use factual statements as a backdrop to our moral arguments (which we need to do), we ought to make sure they are accurate.

The second pillar of good moral reasoning is *consistency*. One of the basic truths of rational discourse is that contradiction is fatal. If a person believes that the sky is blue *and* that the sky is not blue, then he fails the basic test of rationality; we think that he is either deluded or mad. Similarly, we expect people's moral beliefs to be consistent. Someone who thinks that killing is wrong *and* not wrong is irrational in the same way, and we'd be under no pressure to take his views seriously.

This may not seem like a very helpful constraint on argument, since most of the people we come across aren't irrational to this extreme degree. But poor arguments often exhibit inconsistency in less obvious ways. For example, if a government minister has a policy of abolishing private education but sends her children to a for-fee school, then her position is morally inconsistent: she's acting in a way that's wrong according to her own beliefs. In this case, we may suspect that she is blinded by her desire that her own child have the best education possible, and that prudential concerns have therefore trumped her moral ones. Similarly, if a student spends his evenings downloading copyrighted material from the internet for entertainment and then complains when someone plagiarizes his essay to get a top mark at school, he has been morally inconsistent: he had different moral responses to actions that, ostensibly at least, have the same moral ramifications.

Lots of moral argument in the real world turns on this issue of consistency, and I include many examples of this later in the book. Here, we might consider the following:

A: I believe the debts that poor countries owe to international lenders should be cancelled.
B: So do you believe the debts that poor individuals owe to banks ought to be cancelled too?
A: No. Individuals should pay their debts.
B: Then so should poor countries. You're being inconsistent.

In this hypothetical exchange, *A* has to prove that there's a morally relevant difference between poor individuals and poor countries, or his argument fails the consistency test. There may be many such differences for him to draw on, but until they're articulated, his reasoning is poor, and *B* is under no obligation to adopt his conclusion. As we'll see, failure to consider questions of consistency can be a real problem in moral thinking about aid and development.

The third test for moral reasoning is possibly the most important, but it's also the hardest to quantify. A good moral argument should somehow exemplify a *good will*. This idea is frustratingly imprecise (perhaps irreducibly so), but I'll try to demonstrate what I mean by way of a counterexample. In Chapter 1, we discussed a situation of appalling deprivation and squalor affecting the lives of millions of people around the world through no fault of their own. Suppose that someone's response to this state of affairs is 'I don't care'. The suffering of the world's poor means nothing to her, whose only concern is that her own quality of life is maintained to an adequate standard. She is as indifferent to the plight of the developing world as she is to every other ethical issue. While she may not live her life in a wantonly destructive way, she does live it in a purely selfish manner. In short, she is an 'amoralist'.

Now, it's possible that she has an incomplete grasp of the facts and just doesn't appreciate the scale of the problem. It's also possible that she is arguing from an inconsistent position, and that she really does care about some things that mean she ought to care about the plight of the poor. However, it's also possible that she's made no such mistake. She may be completely aware of the facts and be arguing from an entirely consistent standpoint. In this case, her position satisfies our first two tests for moral argument, even though it looks like this led to a very stark and selfish conclusion. The amoralist demonstrates why proper moral thinking can't just be about facts and consistency – it must also be about wanting the *right* kind of things.

This admittedly vague idea is what I mean when I say that good moral argument needs to exemplify a good will. Somehow, proper moral thinking needs not only to be rational but also to demonstrate virtuous intent on the part of the arguer. This idea of a 'good' will or having the 'right' set of dispositions is the most contentious and difficult part of ethical theory. It involves intractable ideas, such as subjectivity, desire and emotion, all of which are notoriously hard to fit into a proper moral theory with any kind of rigour. As a result, I'm going to defer the discussion of what kinds of virtue might be helpful in moral reasoning until the next chapter, when I look at two concepts which seem to me to be indispensable.

The rest of this chapter is instead devoted to some of the more basic questions of moral theory: Who should be the subject of our moral deliberations? What kinds of actions count as properly moral? How should we make our decisions? To kick off this discussion, we'll return to the person who claimed she didn't care about the plight of the poor.

## THE AMORALIST

The amoralist is an extreme character type, but one that's far from impossible to imagine. You may even know someone who claims to hold such a position. Are there any rational means at our disposal with which to persuade such a person that these views are inadequate? Can those who say they are unmoved by moral issues be somehow persuaded to see the unsatisfactory nature of this position? Is there, in fact, anything wrong with this attitude?

Some philosophers believe that there are good reasons not to be completely selfish. In his masterpiece of political philosophy, *Republic*, Plato imagines a discussion between two characters, Socrates and Glaucon. The latter has a hyper-cynical view of morality. Glaucon's position is that there are no reasons to care about such concepts as justice and equality except for superficial social pressure. No rational person would be moral if they could get away with it – the only reason people profess to care about the plight of the world's poor, for example, is the disapprobation they'd attract for expressing a contrary view.

> People do wrong whenever they think they can, so they act morally only if they're forced to, because they regard morality as something which isn't good for one personally. The point is that everyone thinks the rewards of immorality far outweigh those of morality – and they're right.[3]

Given the obvious advantages of being selfish, it's perfectly rational and sensible for people to be as immoral as they can get away with. If we're to believe Glaucon, then there's nothing wrong with the amoralist – she's just articulating a position that we'd all adopt if we were in a position to.

There are a number of ways of responding to the amoralist. The first is to take what she says at face value and accept that she really has *no* moral feelings at all. In this case, there might be some value in trying to expound the benefits of living morally. This is the general approach that Socrates takes in *Republic*, arguing that, despite appearances, the moral person actually enjoys a far better quality of life than the immoral person. The amoralist might derive short-term benefits from being maximally selfish, but the moral person takes a far richer and more profound pleasure from acting ethically. One of Socrates' points is that there is something *essentially* moral about human beings, and that acting in accordance with our true nature (or purpose) is the only source of lasting satisfaction. The pleasures and benefits of living a purely selfish existence are, if not entirely illusory, then certainly much less fulfilling than those acquired by behaving virtuously.

This kind of argument may seem quite appealing. Most of us do have a vague feeling that acting ethically leads to a sense of well-being. If we acted selfishly all the time, ever maximizing our own pleasure at the expense of everyone else's, then we would end up living a dry, shrivelled kind of life. We'd be shutting ourselves off from the pleasures of knowing that we act in accordance with our better nature. Being sensitive to the deprivation suffered by the world's poorest, we may think, is something that we can take satisfaction in and that ultimately leads to our having a better, richer life.

Now this may all be true, but it rather misses the point of the amoralist's challenge. She can accept that *you* wouldn't take a profound and nuanced satisfaction from a purely selfish life, but she disagrees with the claim that *she* is subject to those kinds of motivations. Perhaps the reason you wouldn't enjoy behaving amorally is down to the guilt you'd feel, or the worry you'd have that your pleasures are more fleeting and shallow than those of others. If you don't have those nagging worries (as the amoralist claims not to), maybe you'd really enjoy a life of selfishness and amorality. And there's no doubt that the amoralist, by not being encumbered with the obligation to donate money or time to those less fortunate, does accumulate a lot of things that make her happy.

So it's quite hard to make Socrates' argument stick. If someone really doesn't care about their fellow human beings at all, then it's difficult to argue them into doing so by appealing to the benefits of the moral life – they can simply deny that they'd be any happier than they are already.

An alternative approach to the challenge the amoralist poses is outlined by the philosopher Bernard Williams. He tries to imagine what a person who claims to be an 'amoralist' would be like. If such people *genuinely* have no concern for anyone but themselves, then that would make them psychologically quite odd. Even people who behave extremely badly usually have some level of care (or empathy or protectiveness) towards some individuals. Williams mentions the stereotypical movie gangster, who is ruthless towards almost everybody but still loves his mother. Although such characters claim to be *amoral*, they are actually just very *immoral*: they do care about some individuals in a moral sense, just not very many. If we discover that our amoralist is genuinely incapable of empathizing with others, then we'd have to conclude that she is a psychopath, and trying to argue rationally with a psychopath might well be a waste of time.[4]

Williams' point is that even the most immoral people have some things or people that they care about. At the very least, they are able to understand what it would be like to do something for somebody else. If we want to encourage amoralists to be better people, the task is not, as Socrates believed, to show them how to shift into an entirely different 'moral' life, but to show how similar their existing moral preoccupations are to those that we have and encourage her to incorporate this wider range of subjects into her moral imagination:

> If we can get him [the amoralist] to extend his sympathies to less
> immediate persons who need help, we might be able to do it for less
> immediate persons whose interests have been violated, and so get
> him to have some primitive grasp on notions of fairness. If we can get
> him all this way, then, while he has no doubt an extremely shaky hold
> on moral considerations, he has some hold on them; at any rate, he is
> not the amoralist we started with.[5]

So one response to the person who claims to feel no level of compassion for other people is to show them what the true implications of that claim are. If she's really unable to feel any vestige of
responsibility for anyone else, then she's ceased to be anything
more than a psychopath. If, however, she only cares about a very
narrow range of things, then we might well be able to persuade
her to consider expanding her horizons a little.

## THE SCOPE OF MORALITY

A true amoralist is a rare and strange beast. It's much more common to come across the second type of person: someone who
indeed cares about *some* things, but only those that are close to
home. Such a person might feel compassion for those around
him, like his family and friends, but not for those much further
afield. If he lives in the affluent north of the planet, the concerns
of the poor south may seem too distant to register. He may live a
personal life of relative generosity and probity, but his moral radar
doesn't extend any further than those whom he comes into contact with on a fairly regular basis.

This position may not seem a lot better than the previous one.
Expressed baldly, it seems selfish and narrow-minded. However,
aside from its being far more common than the extreme example
of the amoralist, it's also not clear that any of us is immune from it.

Philosophers love to illustrate contentious moral ideas with wildly implausible examples, so let's use one here.

Suppose you return home from work to find your house is on fire. You only have time to save one person from the flames before it collapses. There are two people within: your aged mother who raised you from an infant and a man you've never met before who'd come round to sell a set of encyclopaedias.[6] Now, it's possible that you would choose to rescue the travelling salesman, but my guess is that most of us would save the beloved relative first. In such a desperate situation, we place a much higher priority on those closest to us, and it's unclear that we're wrong to do so. If someone rushed to save the salesman first, we wouldn't normally find them praiseworthy – we'd think they were crazy or that there had been some deep family feud. Human society is structured around relationships of trust and dependence, and our moral responses are indelibly linked to them. It would be unusual for us to give the same moral weight to anonymous individuals whom we've had no previous contact with than we'd give to those we have regular associations with and bonds of affection to.[7]

Does this mean that we shouldn't care as much about those distant from us? One philosopher who's challenged this idea is Peter Singer. He's probably best known for his arguments for extending moral significance to animals,[8] but he has also written widely and influentially on the question of the relative moral weight given to human members of a distant nation or culture.

Let's consider Singer's basic ethical position. He takes seriously the idea that our moral intuitions (our instinctive, or 'pre-theoretical' views on what to do) are rooted in our early socio-biological development. We have a strong motivation to preserve ourselves, of course, but even in the earliest social groups there were other factors at work. There are evolutionary advantages to members of a social group occasionally putting aside their individual interests to advance a common goal. In the long run, this behaviour benefits the individual more than purely selfish behaviour would have done, and the whole community prospers too.

In the early stages of human development, this cooperative behaviour was instinctive, driven by our environmental needs or our genetics. However, as our brains grew and society moved into a more enlightened phase, we began to use our ability to reason to consider our actions in a more abstract manner. As society becomes more complex, it becomes important for individuals within a group to *defend* their behaviour in a rational way. In order for this process to work, the individual has to be able to place himself in the positions of those around him. After all, why would his peers accept a moral justification if it didn't in some way include their interests too? To be effective, the reasoning used to defend a course of action has to be *impartial*. As Singer puts it:

> In making ethical decisions I am trying to make decisions which can be defended to others. This requires me to take a perspective from which my own interests count no more, simply because they are my own, than the similar interests of others.[9]

Initially, the interests of the immediate community are the only ones that matter. We are familiar with stories from history of communities having very partial and exclusive views of moral significance – so it's possible, for example, for the Israelites of the Old Testament to have thought it was wrong to enslave each other but acceptable to enslave other nations; and Plato didn't like the idea of Greeks laying waste to the lands of other Greeks but was perfectly happy with such things happened to non-Greeks. The problem with the principal of impartiality, though, is that, as moral reasoning moves further away from the particular to the abstract, it becomes increasingly hard to see why 'outsiders' shouldn't deserve the same moral considerations as 'insiders'. By the nineteenth century, most Greeks would have rejected the standards of their ancient forebears and included all fellow Europeans as objects of moral consideration. They might not, however, have extended the same courtesy to Africans – as it happened, the scope of moral significance had widened from the immediate community, to the nation–state, to the racial group.

Singer's point is that if we take morality to be an essentially impartial and rational process, then this process will keep going. The number of individuals to be considered morally significant will keep expanding until we run up against some objective reason why a certain group can't be included:

> The circle of altruism has broadened from the family and tribe to the nation and race, and we are beginning to recognise that our obligations extend to all human beings. [. . .] The only justifiable stopping place for the expansion of altruism is the point at which all whose welfare can be affected by our actions are included within the circle of altruism.[10]

For Singer, there is a simple test for whether something is worthy of moral consideration. If that thing has a concept of its own suffering – in other words, if it's sentient – and we're in a position to affect its welfare, then we have a moral responsibility towards it. That means that all people – and any sentient animals – come within the expanding circle of altruism.

This view of ethics makes a fairly stringent demand on our moral sensibility. Singer thinks that we have an absolute responsibility to transfer resources and effort from the rich world to the poor world, unless doing so would involve us in some other kind of moral transgression. It doesn't matter how far away from us those people are, or whether we have any kind of cultural connection with them. If we own more resources than we need to subsist, and others are in a state of desperate want, then we are morally obliged to assist them. In his paper 'Famine, Affluence, and Morality', he states the argument like this:

> If I am walking past a shallow pond and see a child drowning in it, I ought to wade in and pull the child out. This will mean getting my clothes muddy, but this is insignificant, while the death of the child would presumably be a very bad thing. [. . .] It makes no moral difference whether the person I can help is a neighbour's child ten yards from me or a Bengali whose name I shall never know, ten thousand miles away. [. . .] If it is in our power to prevent something very bad

from happening, without thereby sacrificing anything morally significant, we ought, morally, to do it.[11]

Singer's position is simple: there is no morally relevant difference
between helping someone close to hand and helping someone
thousands of miles away. As morality is an impartial business, a
European is as much obliged to devote time and effort to poverty
in distant countries as she would be among her own community.
This obligation lasts as long as there are significant differences of
wealth in the world, and applies to everyone with the power to
affect the balance of welfare. If it's immoral not to pull the child
from the pond, it's also immoral not to help the starving child in
Bengal. Distance is the only factor separating the two cases, and,
according to Singer, it's irrelevant.

This argument is an uncomfortable one. Taken to its conclusion, almost none of us will ever live up to the demands that it
places on us. This is because Singer believes that we should
stop working to alleviate the suffering of the world's poor only
when giving any more would increase our own suffering beyond
the degree of those we are trying to help. To return to the hypothetical example above, I shouldn't stop trying to rescue the
drowning child just because I am getting cold or because my
suit is expensive and I don't want to ruin it – I should only stop
if I am myself in danger of drowning. In the same way, our moral
obligation to the world's poor only discharges once we've
stripped our lives of all the unnecessary luxuries that adorn it,
and we're only left with those things that meet our basic
needs.

Such a scenario might seem wildly unrealistic to you. Any
moral theory that demands we give the same moral weight to a
drowning child in front of our eyes and starving children thousands of miles away would demand a truly radical change of
behaviour on the part of everyone in the rich world. We'd have to
stop regarding charitable donations as praiseworthy, and see
them as insultingly inadequate responses. Assisting the global

poor would assume an importance far exceeding the level it currently has. You might think that it's so outlandish that it couldn't
possibly be taken seriously.

But if the thesis doesn't appeal to you, it can't be rejected just
because it seems outlandish. If we're serious about deciding how
far our moral responsibilities extend, then we need some *reasons*
as to why Singer's account can't be the whole story.

## MORAL SAINTS

If we wanted to argue against Singer's idea of the equivalence
between saving the child in the pool and the child starving in
Bengal, we could do it by showing that there is something amiss
with the example. Perhaps it's a false equivalence: there really *is* a
morally relevant distinction we can draw on that shows why we're
obliged to drop everything to help the drowning child but not
the starving one. Or, maybe the cases are equivalent, but there's
some other reason for not adopting Singer's stringent morality:
perhaps doing so would be too impractical or have perverse
consequences.

There are plenty of responses to Singer in the philosophical
literature,[12] and I consider a couple of them here. One idea is this:
Singer's example makes sense only when considered from an
impartial perspective. As we've seen, he thinks that morality has
progressed in steps from a community-centred system of action
regulation to a concept that embraces all humans equally, and
that the decisions we make must be assessed using a kind of
impersonal calculus. Perhaps this is a faulty view of morality.
Maybe our moral thinking is essentially self-centred. By this, I
don't mean to suggest that it is *selfish*, just that there's something
irreducibly important about judging things from a particular
perspective (our own) rather than from a disembodied objective
standpoint. Singer himself considers the case of radical child-
rearing practices in the early kibbutzim, where parents were

supposed to treat all children of the community equally and give their own progeny no special consideration. These strictures proved impossible to maintain: the moral ties between close family members were too strong. Mothers crept into the dormitories at night to look after their own offspring. Can anyone really maintain that they were *wrong* to do so?

In a related case, let's imagine the kind of person who gives no consideration at all to her own well-being (beyond basic subsistence needs), weighs every moral decision in terms of the objective good it will do to others, and never acts unless these tests are satisfied. Every temptation to do something she likes (such as going to a play, or eating a nice meal) is met with the response, 'But if I used the money to alleviate the suffering of the most disadvantaged in the world, it would be better spent'. So that's what she does. This unlikely individual represents the extreme of Singer's thesis. There may even be people in the world who live like this – they'd be opposite to the amoralists we looked at earlier – 'super-moralists'. If this is true, though, could we regard their existence as a good thing? Would we respect them, and want to be around them? Or would they seem to have lost some quality essential to their engagement with society?

In her paper, 'Moral Saints', Susan Wolf discusses such an individual:

> If the moral saint is devoting all his time to feeding the hungry or healing the sick or raising money for Oxfam, then necessarily he is not reading Victorian novels, playing the oboe, or improving his backhand. Although none of the interests or tastes in the category containing the latter activities could be claimed to be a necessary element in a life well lived, a life in which *none* of these possible aspects of character are developed may seem to be a life strangely barren.[13]

The problem, for Wolf, with being a 'moral saint', is that all other worthwhile pursuits are relegated to the status of unimportant frivolities. If everything is subjected to the test of how much welfare it promotes, then much else that is important and valuable will be lost. Of course, she doesn't suggest that we should *ignore* the demands of morality, just that morality isn't the only thing we ought to be worried about. Indeed, by privileging impartial moral concerns to the exclusion of all others, we risk losing all the other good things in our lives, and end up living a barren existence. We can admire the person who turns aside from a generous and flourishing life to save a drowning child, since that person displays the full range of admirable virtues, but we have little time for the pious individual whose entire existence is devoted to sending food parcels to Bengal and whose intellectual and social life, as a consequence, has withered on the vine.

I discuss this idea of 'character virtues' in the next chapter, when we look at alternative moral theories. Here, another idea we devote some time to is 'rights', which sits uneasily with Singer's outlook too. Consider a community of people, the Ants, who work hard and forgo significant short-term pleasures in exchange for long-term prosperity. They live adjacent to another community, the Grasshoppers, who make no such provision for the future, and hence fall on hard times. As the years pass, those hard times turn into desperate times, and the Grasshoppers are reduced to penury. Now, it may be that the kind-hearted Ants feel moved to assist the Grasshoppers. If they did so, it would be very nice of them. But are they morally obliged to?

It's unclear that they are, at least to the extent that Singer describes. Surely, it's up to the Ants whether they give away the things that they've worked to accumulate. As John Arthur writes in 'Famine Relief and the Ideal Moral Code':

> Equal consideration seems to require that we should prevent harm to others if in doing so we do not sacrifice anything of comparable moral importance. But there is another idea [. . .]: the idea of entitlements – that I have rights or may justly deserve something – and these are also morally significant.[14]

I don't mean to suggest that the poorest people in the world have become so through laziness like the Grasshoppers, nor that the rich world has accumulated its riches through blameless hard work (as we've seen, that's hardly the case). The point is that our entitlements – the things we've worked for, the rights we have to flourish and enjoy the benefits of our success – are not morally negligible. When we're deciding how much weight to put on the suffering of those we have no ready emotional connection to, these elements must be placed into the mix. To do otherwise is to reduce moral decision making to a calculus of outcomes that has no grounding in our experience as human beings. As Arthur puts it:

> While we do care about others' wellbeing, we care especially about those we love, and we also care deeply about our own lives. It will therefore be difficult, to put it mildly, to get people to accept and support a code requiring that they give away their savings [. . .] to a stranger simply because to do so would avoid substantial evil.[15]

The criticism here is that Singer's account of morality is too simple. Things like rights to property, possessions and a family life also have a relevant place in our moral deliberations. Such rights would not be threatened by my wading into a shallow pool to save a child, but they would be threatened if I were expected to devote all my non-essential resources to helping the world's poor.

So, where does this discussion leave us? You'll have to make up your own mind about Singer's challenge, of course, but I'll offer a couple of thoughts. Singer's account is very good at explaining why no particular set of individuals should be exempt from our moral consideration. He's right to say that limiting our altruism to those in our immediate community is no longer acceptable (if it ever was), and he's also right when he claims that any properly enlightened moral system involves some element of impartiality and even-handedness. So the tragedy affecting the world's poor *ought* to provoke us into action, and we do have some level of duty to do something about it.

At the same time, this duty needs to be placed against the pressing moral obligations we have to those very close to us (our family and friends) as well as our legitimate human desire to flourish and prosper as individuals. This is true both for reasons of practicality (any ethical theory needs to be realistic about the demands it places on us), and also because it properly reflects the full spectrum of our moral lives.

What we're left with, then, is a need to find a balance between two competing intuitions: the desire to take care of ourselves (to a reasonable degree) and the desire to improve the conditions affecting the world's worst off (to a reasonable degree). What we need now is a means of determining where to draw the line, a way to judge what level of engagement is reasonable. It might be helpful to have some kind of independent test or decision process that would help us figure out how to get the balance right. We'll take a look at one such mechanism in the next chapter. Before we get to that, however, we need to look at another complication in our moral thinking about aid.

## ACTS AND OMISSIONS

When we're thinking about the right way to live our lives, we normally couch our arguments in terms of the kinds of *actions* we ought to perform. So the vexing questions of applied ethics usually take the form, 'Is it ever right to abort a foetus?' or 'Is it ever right to kill someone in order to end their suffering?' What we occasionally forget is that as well as making decisions to act in one way or another, we also implicitly *refrain* from doing lots of things that we conceivably could do. Although these omissions don't attract as much attention, some of them end up having a much greater effect on other people.

Our engagement with the developing world is a good example of this. Most of us would think it wrong of me to stop writing this book, head out into the street and kill someone before returning to my desk to carry on typing. However, if I do not give £20 to Oxfam this morning, it's possible a child in Africa will die of malnutrition. It is certainly true that if, over my lifetime, I had chosen to give more money or time to charitable causes, then some lives would have been saved. My failure to act has had exactly the same moral consequences as walking out into the street with a shotgun – at least one person has died. If I really do go out and shoot someone, there is no doubt that I have behaved in a morally improper way. And yet, if I choose to keep writing this book rather than rushing out to donate money to Oxfam, we don't think that I've done anything remotely as bad. As Phillipa Foot writes,

> Most of us allow people to die of starvation in India and Africa, and there is surely something wrong with us that we do; it would be nonsense, however, to pretend that it is only in law that we make a distinction between allowing people in the underdeveloped countries to die of starvation and sending them poisoned food.[16]

The idea here is that there's a morally relevant difference between acting and omitting to act, even if the consequences are, in moral terms, exactly the same.

But is this right? Should we feel as guilty over our lack of action to prevent death and suffering as we would do over a deliberate decision to inflict it on someone? It's a surprisingly difficult problem and makes itself felt across a number of different areas of ethics. You may be familiar with the idea advanced by some doctors and lawyers that there's a distinction to be made between killing someone and allowing them to die.[17] In a similar way, we might worry about the difference between flying out to Uganda with the intention of murdering twenty people (definitely wrong), and keeping funds in our possession that would have saved twenty lives (less wrong, surely, but why?).

Once again, we'll have to work to find some reasons why the two cases are different if we want to avoid the uncomfortable idea that there's a strong moral equivalence between acts and omissions. If we can't find good enough reasons, then we'll have to accept that our omissions are morally important, which would entail a radical change in our way of life (just as Singer's thesis would). And there are indeed a number of ways in which we could attempt to show why the two cases are different.

First, in the situation when I head out to Uganda to kill twenty people I have a definite intention to do harm, whereas when I refrain from sending money to assist starving people I simply haven't thought about the issue. I wish the potential Ugandan recipients of my money no ill will, it's just that they haven't registered on my radar – I'm ignorant of their plight in a way that I couldn't be if I'd specifically planned to kill them. For this reason, runs the argument, there is a significant moral difference between the act and the omission. In the first case, I know perfectly well what I'm doing and to whom, whereas in the latter case I have no such knowledge of the facts – I may not even know where Uganda is or that there's any problem with food supply there. As a result, I can't be blamed if I don't send food there, even if people die.

Now there are certainly cases where ignorance of the facts is a good defence. If I really don't know about something – a plot by gangsters to rob a bank, say – then I can't be held responsible for anything I fail to do with respect to it. This doesn't quite get us out of the bind, however. We have the privilege of living in a society where information is widespread. It would be very difficult for someone with even a basic level of education not to know that there are those in the developing world at risk of death or suffering in the absence of intervention. The supposition that we have no idea of the effects of withholding our aid is not very convincing – we *do* have an idea of what the consequences of inaction are, but we don't like to think about them very often.

Moreover, even if we are genuinely ignorant of global economic reality, there are times when ignorance is no defence. It's plausible to claim that we have a responsibility to find out about what's going on in the world, and that failure to do so is a moral short-coming. The England cricketer Mike Gatting, when facing criticism for breaking a boycott on touring apartheid-era South Africa, defended himself by claiming that he didn't know very much about the issues. It was a poor defence – he *ought* to have known.[18] In the same way, we ought not to be ignorant of the suffering in the developing world, and once we know the facts, the moral distinction between 'killing' and 'letting die' seems less sure.

Someone who wanted to maintain the distinction between acts and omissions might point out another relevant factor here. In the case of murder, I know exactly who I'm going to kill. I might even look them in the eye as I pull the trigger. That level of certainty means I can't escape responsibility for my actions. In the case of failing to send money to Uganda, though, I have no idea which twenty people will die. I don't know where they live or what their names are, and I have no idea when their suffering will terminate their lives. In practical terms, it's probably impossible for me to know with certainty *which* twenty people died as a result of my not sending the money. So I'm less culpable – the vagueness of the consequences means I can't be held morally responsible.

Again, it's a strange defence. The idea that we need to have some kind of clarity about the effects of our actions (or omissions) in order to be responsible for them doesn't stand up to much scrutiny. Take the example of a terrorist bomber. He might not know anything about his victims. He might set his bomb to go off at a random point in a busy street at a random time, and have no determinate idea of who will get killed by it. The fact that he hasn't picked out particular individuals doesn't excuse his actions. In the same way, the fact that I don't know *which* Ugandans will die of starvation, or when, doesn't absolve me of the responsibility to send the money to stop it happening. If I know that my funds could prevent that suffering, I ought to send them.

At this point, you may be more frustrated with philosophical argument than with the question at hand. *Of course* there's a difference between actively murdering people and allowing people to die through inaction, you may think. The point, though, is that we have to establish some kind of relevant *reason* for there being a difference if we're to be sure that our intuitions are correct. It may be that failing to send aid to the developing world really is a moral crime on the same level as murder, and it's only our laziness and lack of imagination that prevents us from seeing it. If that were so, then we'd have to change the way we live, and take the issue of poor-country suffering a lot more seriously. And so far, the reasons we've come up with to separate the two cases haven't been very persuasive.

There is one defence, though, that does at least water down the radical conclusion that acts and omissions are morally equivalent, and it's similar to the one we discussed in the last section. Our actions are finite: there are only so many things we can do in our lifetime. Our omissions, on the other hand, are infinite: we'd never be able to assess the consequences of all the things we could have done but didn't. As a result, it's just not practical to worry about all the courses we hypothetically might have taken – we should concentrate on the things we've actually done or plan to do. Anyone insane enough to try to assess all the potential missed opportunities for doing good would drive herself into an early grave, overwhelmed by the scale of her moral shortcomings.

This is undoubtedly true, and it's a powerful reason for thinking that we can't treat all our omissions to act on the same level as our actions. This, however, only takes us so far. The above cases show the extent to which actions and omissions are troublingly close in moral terms. Though we may not like the consequences very much, there *is* a worrying similarity between the active murder of people and the withholding of financial assistance that leads to their deaths. Though there are practical reasons we're unlikely to treat the cases as being exactly the same, if we took the similarities a bit more seriously, then we might be inclined to take a more active interest in relieving the plight of the world's poorest. As Jonathan Glover, a philosopher with a sceptical view of the acts/omissions distinction, writes,

Although there are substantial differences of side-effects, deliberately failing to send money to Oxfam, without being able to justify our

alternative spending as more important, is in the same league as murder. If this is so, a lot of us are living far below the moral standards we
believe in. To deny the acts and omissions doctrine is [therefore] to
propose a radical and very demanding morality.[19]

Glover has a very sophisticated discussion of acts and omissions
in his book, *Causing Death and Saving Lives*, and I recommend taking a look at it if this topic interests you.[20] Although there are some
important qualifications, he essentially argues, persuasively in my
view, that killing someone and letting them die when we have the
power to prevent it are on more or less the same level.

If this is true, then we're faced with a real challenge: if we think
murder is wrong, and if inactivity in the face of world poverty is a
morally similar issue, then why aren't we doing *more* to prevent
the deaths and suffering of people whom we can plausibly help?
Of course, saying that 'something must be done' and coming up
with the correct course of action are two very different things. As
you've no doubt observed, I have assumed throughout this discussion that simple actions such as giving money to Oxfam are
unambiguously the 'right' thing to do. In fact, as we'll discover in
later chapters, it's often very unclear how resources, time and
expertise can be deployed to best effect, and in the real world,
matching up good intentions to good outcomes is a frustratingly
opaque business.

However, there are some general considerations that might
help us in framing a response. We mentioned earlier that it would
be nice to have a procedure for making decisions that would help
us in our ethical quandaries. Philosophers have spent a lot of time
thinking about producing theories that could help guide us to
the right kinds of outcomes, and we'll take a look at the most
influential of them in the following chapter.

# 3 Compassion and Justice

We've spent some time looking at the basis of our moral thinking about aid and development. I've argued that there is a strong moral pressure on us to do *something* about the scale of world poverty, and that we can't easily hide behind the excuse that the victims are too far away or that there's an important difference between acts and omissions. Throughout the discussion, though, we've been dealing with very simple ideas about what counts as a good action (giving money to Oxfam, for example, or going to Africa to help with famine relief). If things were really that simple, then our task would be very easy indeed – we'd just commit to those basic actions that would relieve the world of suffering and move on to the next big problem. Sadly, things are much more complicated than that. There's a huge variety of ways in which a member of the rich world – an individual or a country – might choose to help a member of the poor world, and it's not always obvious how to choose among them. In addition, a growing critical consensus in the media often points to the occasions when well-intentioned actions end up having bad consequences or aid money is squandered through alleged corruption and waste in both the donor and recipient countries.[1]

We'll look at how the aid industry operates in more detail in Chapters 4 and 5, which are concerned with the practical side of attempts to tackle global poverty. In the rest of this chapter, we'll stay with ethical theory but move the focus of our enquiry from the conceptual basis of our moral thinking to the 'active' side: how we might choose between various aid options. I don't attempt to give a hard-and-fast formula for action, but merely sketch some of the considerations we might like to bear in mind. I do suggest, though, that any choice we make has to pass three basic tests.

First, it has to demonstrate the good will that we talked about in Chapter 2. Second, it should be compatible with the demands of justice. Third, it should produce the best possible consequences, subject to some reasonable constraints. Taken together, these three goals still leave plenty of room for divergent approaches to aid and development, but they do at least direct our thoughts in a broad, hopefully helpful, direction. To begin with, we'll take a look at the last idea on that list – the importance of consequences.

## UTILITY

Utilitarianism is an ethical model first proposed by the British philosophers Jeremy Bentham (1748–1832) and John Stuart Mill (1806–1873).[2] Prior to their work, morality was seen by most Europeans primarily as a matter of religious interpretation. There were disputes about moral issues of course, but the mechanism for resolving them generally involved an attempt to discern God's will or an appeal to established norms. Scepticism about the link between morality and religion emerged in the writers of the Enlightenment, notably David Hume. Bentham's and Mill's utilitarianism was radical, though, in its attempt to ground a theory of moral action purely in natural, rather than supernatural, properties.

For both Bentham and Mill, an action is right or wrong depending on how much 'utility' it creates or destroys. Utility has been conceived in a number of ways: in the earliest conception of the theory, it was basically synonymous with 'pleasure', but the notion was subsequently refined to include richer concepts, such as 'well-being'. The essential point to note is that, whatever value we assign to 'utility', the rightness of an action depends *entirely* on how well the action promotes or degrades it. In other words, the consequences of an action are the important moral factors. Utilitarianism is thus a variety of 'consequentialist' theory.[3]

This idea may seem blindingly obvious to you. Why on earth *wouldn't* the consequences of an action determine its moral status? If you feel like this, part of the reason is the success of utilitarianism in entering the public consciousness. It's the dominant theory used to justify moral choices, particularly in professions where resource allocation is the primary problem (such as health care, welfare distribution and the delivery of international aid). This is no accident, since some variety of utilitarian theory is indeed very useful in helping us decide what to do about a difficult problem like eradicating world poverty. However, as I hope to show, it's not the only way of thinking through moral choices, and in its crudest form, it can lead to outcomes that are far from those originally intended.

Let's start with the theory at its simplest, again using very basic examples of aid donation. I have £20 burning a hole in my pocket and can spend it in a number of ways. I can go to the cinema with my wife, and probably have change for a drink afterwards. Or I can donate it to an aid agency, which will use the money to help impoverished villagers in Zambia. If I'm a good utilitarian, I'll make my decision based on how much utility is generated by my actions. For the purposes of this example, let's take 'well-being' as our species of utility: I'll use the £20 to promote as much well-being as I can.

Given that this is the only consideration, it seems right that I should give the £20 to the Zambian villagers. I like going to the cinema, but I do it quite a lot, so my well-being will only be increased marginally if I choose this option. However, the same sum of money could provide significant improvements to the Zambians' quality of life (perhaps a substantial amount of food, say). Their well-being will be improved far in excess of mine, so the utilitarian calculus yields the result that I should forgo my cinema trip and send the money to Africa.

In very simple examples like this, utilitarianism seems helpful enough. It can serve to focus my mind on the relative importance of various kinds of goods. We could imagine the process being scaled up to help in the distribution of more serious sums of money. An aid agency director might have £2 million to spend in a variety of ways. After doing some research, it becomes apparent that poor sanitation is the greatest cause of suffering in his target country. Spending the majority of the cash on improving sanitation will generate the greatest amount of well-being, so that's where the money goes. Decisions like that take place all the time, and it certainly seems a rational enough way of going about things.

Scratch the surface, however, and things get rather more difficult. We've been treating 'well-being' so far as something that can be easily measured and compared. This may be true enough when we're looking at a choice between a cinema ticket and the relief of starvation, but in most cases, things won't be nearly as clear cut. The example of the aid agency director with £2 million to spend is laughably crude. In the real world, the poor official will probably have to weigh many competing priorities, each capable of delivering different amounts of well-being. If we take a look at the UK government's spending priorities for Malawi in 2009, we can see the wide range of choices on offer:[4]

|                               | Spend in £m | |
| Area                          | 2006/7 | 2010/11 |
| --- | --- | --- |
| Budget support                | 20     | 26      |
| Growth, including agriculture | 6      | 6       |
| Social protection             | –      | 5       |
| Governance                    | 5      | 6.5     |
| Health and HIV/AIDS           | 21     | 29      |
| Education                     | 6      | 12      |
| Water                         | 0.3    | 0.5     |
| Acute needs                   | 3      | –       |
| Other                         | 3.7    | –       |
| Total                         | 65     | 85      |

We can see, even in this pretty simple list, that there are some changes of priority between 2006/7 and 2010/11: education spending doubles, while 'acute needs' spending is withdrawn entirely. Juggling the various different priorities is a difficult job, and it's not immediately obvious which is the most important area. How could we make an intelligent measure of the respective amounts of 'well-being' generated by, say, the health and education systems? Clearly, the former holds the promise of relieving many people of painful and debilitating illnesses. On the other hand, without an educated populace, the general economy will never progress, and people will remain unaware of their basic civil rights. It would be nice to support both, but if we only have the money to support one aim, or part of each one, how does utilitarianism help us decide what to do?

If there were some way of agreeing on standard units of well-being, and we could reliably predict how many such units would be generated by a particular policy, we might be able to accurately compare the various courses of action to determine which ones we ought to pursue. An idea similar to this was memorably satirized by Michael Frayn in his book, *A Landing on the Sun*, in which a civil servant and a philosopher attempt to define 'quality of life' in a way that would somehow feed into government policy. They end up concluding that it has 'something to do with washing machines' and not getting very much further.[5] Despite the absurdity of Frayn's treatment, though, significant effort is expended by our public bodies in doing exactly that: trying to define 'well-being' in ways that can be compared and measured. As a result, there's a large body of literature in the social sciences devoted to producing a decision-making procedure for resource distribution on broadly utilitarian lines.

One influential example is the Quality-Adjusted Life Year (or QALY). This is used in the health sector to compare the benefits of various interventions. We can start with the idea that a medical or therapeutic process ought to prolong life. If, after conducting some research, we find that a certain policy increases patients' lives by ten years, then that gives us a quantitative value for the utility of pursuing that policy. If another policy increased patients' lives by twenty years, then resources might be allocated in that direction instead. However, it's possible that those twenty years would be filled with unavoidable pain, or require extensive and traumatic surgery. In that case, the number of well-being units would be reduced to take account of this. The 'life years' in question are thus adjusted for 'quality', with the intention of producing a reasonably complete and nuanced accumulation of the projected improvement in well-being. Here's how the UK's National Institute for Clinical Excellence, a body charged with deciding whether new drugs should be available through the National Health Service (NHS), uses them:

> Patient $x$ has a serious, life-threatening condition. If he continues receiving standard treatment he will live for 1 year and his quality of life will be 0.4 (0 or below = worst possible health, 1 = best possible health). If he receives the new drug he will live for 1 year 3 months (1.25 years), with a quality of life of 0.6. The new treatment is compared with standard care in terms of the QALYs gained:
>
> • Standard treatment: 1 (year's extra life) × 0.4 = 0.4 QALY
> • New treatment: 1.25 (1 year, 3 months extra life) × 0.6 = 0.75 QALY
>
> Therefore, the new treatment leads to 0.35 additional QALYs (that is: 0.75 – 0.4 QALY = 0.35 QALYs). The cost of the new drug is assumed to be £10,000, standard treatment costs £3000. The difference in treatment costs (£7000) is divided by the QALYs gained (0.35) to calculate the cost per QALY. So the new treatment would cost £20,000 per QALY.[6]

On the basis of the QALY count, health service directors can plan their interventions in a suitably utilitarian manner.

It's easy to see the attraction of such a scheme. The delivery of aid to poor countries overwhelmingly concerns the transfer of money – either directly or in the form of funding for the services of experts – and sums of money are exactly countable. It's clearly desirable to match the determinate sums being spent with similarly determinable units of output. Ideally, we'd be able to show that $x$ amount of money produces $y$ amount of well-being. The utilitarian calculus would thus be reliable and useful as a guide to action.

Even with such innovations as the QALY, however, we might be sceptical about how far this can go. It should be fairly obvious how a rigid application of such a scheme might lead to difficulties, so I'll only mention a couple of examples. One is the problem of distribution to individuals. Suppose we have a village of a hundred people. Ninety-nine of them have minor problems that can be addressed relatively cheaply. One villager, however, suffers from a chronic illness that's very expensive to treat. Now suppose the amount of money required to help the majority of slightly sick people is the same as that required to help the one very sick one. How should we spend our cash?

It's unclear that a simple version of utilitarianism gives us good answers here. The amount of utility generated would depend on the algorithm we use to determine the improvement in the villagers' welfare. Suppose that the level of suffering experienced by the single individual were so terrible that we ought to erase that, thereby leaving the majority to live with their less-acute symptoms. Although, on some objective scale, we have maximized the sum of possible well-being in the village, it may well seem unfair to the majority that we devoted all the potential resources to helping just one person. However, because the *only* thing that matters in bald utilitarian theories is the outcome – the consequences of actions in terms of well-being – then the majority of villagers have no grounds on which to feel aggrieved.

Another practical problem with utilitarian calculi is time-based. When we are faced with complex real-life decisions, such as those involved in distributing aid, the time it takes for actions to have their effect is a significant complicating factor. To return to the director of our aid agency, she may have £2 million to spend on a whole range of worthy causes. If she had decided to assess the potential utility of her contributions over a five-year period, say,

she might choose to plough all her resources into food distribution and health care, as this will prevent starvation and improve
the quality of life dramatically. At the end of those five years, she'd
have maximized the increase in well-being. However, if she'd
decided to assess the utility over, say, thirty years, she might
choose to spend more of it on education and income-generating
activities, since these hold the promise of greater long-term prosperity. The choice would come down to whether long-term or
short-term goals were thought to be more important. Utilitarianism, in its crudest forms, offers no easy way to differentiate
between these objectives, and so its usefulness as a decision-
making procedure is lessened.

It's possible, of course, that these difficulties could be over-
come. It may be that we can come up with very sophisticated
models of utility that would take account of different possible
types of well-being, the problem of individuals and the complication of setting time limits. In practice, utilitarian models of resource
distribution do try to take account of such factors. However, in
order to employ a better model, we'd need to introduce *new* ideas
into our thinking. We could no longer rely on a very simple model
of measurable consequences. Instead, we'd have to take account
of things like fairness, equity, just deserts and rights. At the very
least, bald utilitarianism can't give us what we need to make the
difficult choices posed by international development. To get a
more complete theory of ethical action, we need to draw on extra
resources.

## JUSTICE

One of the most influential ideas in modern development thinking is called the 'rights-based' approach to aid. This, it seems to
me, was born out of a growing awareness in the 1990s and more
recently that bald utilitarian calculations of aid distribution were
insufficiently alive to the real complexities of resource delivery.

The simplest forms of utilitarian planning ignore other potential human goods, such as people's rights and entitlements (we saw this in Chapter 2 in our discussion of Singer's ideas – he's a theorist with a very strong utilitarian approach). Many modern interventions, mindful of such shortcomings, aim to preserve the basic rights that people ought to enjoy, even if it means that the consequences of poverty alleviation in the short term may not be optimal.

The treatment of HIV and AIDS is a good example of this. Arguably, if *all* we care about is the eradication of the epidemic, anyone with HIV in Africa ought to be cordoned off from his or her colleagues, prevented from working in education or medicine, identified as a risk to the community and shunned by all. This level of stigma-creation might well be effective in reducing infection, since it would limit the opportunities of individuals to come into risky contact with others. However, such an approach would contravene their rights to live a life of dignity and richness. The UN's Universal Declaration of Human Rights enshrines a core set of values guaranteeing rights to work, to associate freely, and not to be arbitrarily discriminated against.[7] So it is that charities working to combat AIDS in Africa generally don't insist on such draconian prevention measures. Indeed, they work very hard to ensure that the human rights of individuals are preserved, and that any attempts to limit the spread of infection are compatible with them.[8]

In other words, modern aid interventions attempt to incorporate concepts such as *fairness* and *justice* into their planning. They do so, moreover, in ways that are not easily captured by a pure utilitarian calculus. As we've seen, there are good reasons for wanting to do this, and they hold out the hope of coming up with a more sophisticated basis for action. If we want to enrich the basic utilitarian ethical model we've already looked at with a commitment to some form of justice, how might we go about doing it? It might seem that 'justice' is one of those ideas that means different things to different people, and that there's no chance of incorporating it into a theory everyone would agree on. In

philosophy, this is indeed the case: there's no complete agreement about what the best 'kind' of justice is or how a moral theory
of action would promote it. However, there has been one important attempt to define the concept of justice which deserves our
attention; indeed, no discussion of modern political philosophy
would be complete without it.

In 1971, the academic philosopher John Rawls published a
book with the rather unassuming title, *A Theory of Justice*. At the
time, political philosophy was in a somewhat moribund state.
Rawls' work, which has since gone through two revised editions,
kindled fresh interest in some very old questions. He was concerned with what a just society would look like: how would it
structure itself, and what would be the rational basis for that structure? The proposals he came up with have been extremely influential in setting the terms for contemporary debates in political
philosophy, including over the issue of the distribution of
resources between the rich world and the poor world.

Rawls' proposal is an example of a 'social contract' theory. This
idea is most famously associated with the French philosopher Jean-
Jacques Rousseau, whose book (entitled, helpfully enough, *The
Social Contract*) postulated an explicit agreement among all members of a society, where all individual rights were given up in return
for a guarantee that the 'general will' of the community would be
enacted. Rousseau's proposal was that there would be a real contract between the members of his well-ordered society, and various
institutions would emerge from that agreement that would guarantee both liberty and equality for all within it.[9] Although Rousseau's
ideas were (and are) very influential, many subsequent critics have
found his advocacy of an explicit contract among members of a
community extremely implausible. The hoops Rousseau needs to
jump through in order to prevent his ideal society from becoming
horribly totalitarian or simply impractical have also struck many as
wildly out of kilter with a reasonable view of human nature.[10]

Rawls, though, supports the idea that we can learn a lot about
justice through the idea of a social contract. Unlike Rousseau,

however, he thinks of the contract as being entirely hypothetical – there's no *actual* meeting of individuals to hammer out the principles of justice; instead, by imagining the state of affairs in which a contract *might* have been drawn up, he derives a picture of how real societies ought to be organized.

This might strike you as an odd idea. How can imagining how persons would react in some kind of fictitious environment help us construct a theory of justice for the real world? In fact, such reasoning is extremely common in everyday life. As a child, when I didn't want to eat broccoli at the dinner table, my parents told me that I ought to force it down because if I'd been born in Africa, I'd be extremely grateful for any food at all. By encouraging me to imagine myself in wholly different circumstances, they hoped that I'd see how privileged my actual position was – eating the broccoli would cease to be a terrible imposition, and instead become an example of how lucky I was. Whether or not their reasoning had an effect on me (I quite like broccoli now, so maybe it did), it's not difficult to think of similar examples where the justice of a situation is appealed to with reference to how things might have been, rather than how they are. The common refrain, 'How would you like it if you were in *her* position?' is the generalized form of such appeals.

What's at work here is the realization that the opportunities and goods we possess in life are far from universally shared – lots of people have very different situations and perspectives. If we're to construct a theory of justice that has some kind of claim over all of us, we should try to take into account as many of those different situations and viewpoints as possible. As we noted in our discussion of Singer's position, good ethical theories have some major element of impartiality in them – without that, we're liable simply to end up with a world view that's worryingly similar to the amoralist's. And one way to see how a theory might be properly impartial is to consider how it would strike other people.

This is Rawls' starting point. If we could come up with a definition of justice that everyone would sign up to in principle, then we could be pretty sure that it had some merit. There wouldn't have to be a *real* contractual process for that concept to gain legitimacy, just an argument showing that any sensible, decent person *would* sign up to it as long as they understood all its provisions.

Even getting people to sign up to a hypothetical contract without imposing some further conditions wouldn't guarantee that the results would be fair, though, since every contractor will be influenced by their prejudices, and by a natural desire to advance themselves. Rawls is perfectly aware of these kinds of factors, and does his best to ensure that such prejudices aren't able to influence the process. He draws up some conditions to equalize things, the first of which is that the contractual agreement take place behind a so-called veil of ignorance. Rawls comes up with a fictional state of affairs which he calls 'the original position'. In this state, each individual has somehow existed prior to their entry into society. While in the original position, they don't know where they'll start out in the real world or have any idea how successful they'll be once in it. As Rawls put it,

> No one knows his place in society, his class position or social status, nor does anyone know his fortune in the distribution of natural assets and abilities, his intelligence, strength, and the like. I shall even assume that the parties do not know their conceptions of the good or their special psychological propensities. The principles of justice are chosen behind a veil of ignorance. This ensures that no one is advantaged or disadvantaged in the choice of principles by the outcome of natural chance or the contingency of social circumstances.[11]

This is a pretty extreme condition to impose on the decision procedure. According to Rawls, people in the original position don't even know what their 'conception of the good' is. By this, he means that we don't have any idea about the specifics of what will make us happy or satisfied in the real world beyond a very small set of attributes. It may be that, in real life, my happiness revolves around owning a particular type of car, playing cricket, or indulging in fine wine. In the original position, I don't know any of that. All I'm allowed to take into account is a set of fundamental goods: liberty to pursue my goals, and a set of basic resources such as food and money. Rawls makes a few more assumptions: that the mythical contractors to this agreement aren't chronically selfish, that they're rational, and that they'd like to see more of those general goods than less. Plenty of people in the real world don't exhibit those characteristics, but that's not important for the purposes of the experiment: Rawls' hypothetical contract only needs to show what would happen if people *were* like that.

If people were placed in this original position and asked to agree on an account of a just society, they would all, according to Rawls, be bound to adopt two broad principles. The first is called the Principle of Liberty:

> Each person is to have an equal right to the most extensive basic liberty compatible with a similar liberty for others.[12]

This idea is relatively easy to understand. Rawls thinks that a just society must guarantee the highest level of liberty to each individual that's compatible with everyone else having the same amount.

The second outcome is a subordinate principle, called the Difference Principle:

> Social and economic inequalities are to be arranged so that they are [. . .] to the greatest benefit of the least advantaged.[13]

This is the principle that's of most interest to us: Rawls thinks that people in the original position would agree to adopt a social order where the least advantaged members of society would be given assistance to bring them up to the point where they can enjoy the full range of basic goods. From then on, inequality would be reduced – perhaps by taxation and welfare legislation, perhaps by more forceful methods – until any further attempts to equalize matters would actually disadvantage the poorest. If Rawls is correct in his prediction, then no party to his imagined social contract would ever want to see a situation where inequality beyond a certain level was allowed to be maintained, and so a just society would be one in which equality is promoted to the greatest extent possible, compatible with the preservation of liberty.[14]

Why is Rawls so confident that the parties to the contract will make such a decision? The answer lies in the model of rationality he assumes that people in the original position will have. Remember, they have no way of knowing what position they'll hold in the real world. If we treat his experiment as working on a global level,[15] then the contractor could end up as a Wall Street tycoon or a penniless villager in Somalia. In fact, ending up poor is more likely than ending up rich, since in the real world, the poor outnumber the rich. While still in the original position, the contractor will probably want to arrange things such that *whatever* position she ends up adopting, her life chances will be reasonably good. She'll want everyone to enjoy a high level of the basic social goods – liberty, food, money, and so on – since, if there were massive areas of deprivation, then she might very well be condemning herself to a life of poverty.

According to Rawls, the only truly just society would be one run according to the principles which anyone in the original position would accept. There are, of course, plenty of critics of this conception of justice. It's not immediately obvious that everyone would agree with Rawls' principles even if they were operating under the veil of ignorance: someone with a temperament conducive to risk taking might be happy to be placed in random position within an unequal world, just on the off chance they they'd end up being one of the lucky minority. There's also doubt over the compatibility of Rawls' principle of liberty and his principle of difference – according to the philosopher Robert Nozick, you can't be genuinely free if you're condemned to live in a society where resources are redistributed on the basis of need, regardless of what any given individual may be entitled to based on their labour and aptitude. Rawls' liberalism strikes some commentators as unacceptably distributionist, and others as insufficiently distributionist, so there's by no means a consensus of agreement over his conclusions.[16]

However, Rawls' approach does starkly illustrate the kinds of issues that ought to be at stake in formulating a properly nuanced theory of justice. If we take Rawls' hypothetical challenge seriously, and imagine that we could just as easily have ended up living in Katine as in the rich world, would we be as happy with the current division of global resources as we are now? If we're not comfortable with that idea, then we ought not to be comfortable with the global order that perpetuates such division of resources either. If, by some magical process, we were given the opportunity to choose how the world ought to be arranged *before* we entered it, would we really be happy to place so many people into abject poverty while the planet's resources were so abundant? After all, we could have ended up in their position.

It should be noted here that Rawls' position, as outlined in *A Theory of Justice*, does not address the global situation. His is a theory about how individual societies ought to be ordered, not how the whole world should be run. One of the reasons for this is that states (or 'peoples') are generally seen as the primary agents of justice in the world. It's states that enact laws, levy taxes, and have the power to hold their citizens to account. Rawls' own theory of international justice is rather different to his treatment of domestic justice, and is tolerant of the idea that there can be wide disparities of opportunity and affluence across the globe.[17] However, there are a number of theorists who doubt whether the sharp legal distinction between states and individuals is helpful, or even that it can be meaningfully maintained. The world, as we'll discuss in more detail in Chapter 5, is increasingly governed by international institutions. People are often free to move from one jurisdiction to another (whether legally or illegally), and many important resources (such as fish stocks in international waters) are not 'owned' by any state at all. In recent years, the idea of international justice has become increasingly important, and the notion that national governments are the only (or even primary) source of justice has been challenged.[18]

Though Rawls' ideas are unlikely to be applicable to the global situation, at least without modification, it seems to me that the key idea – that a just social order is one that people would agree to be a part of if they didn't know their place within it prior to 'entering' it – is something that we can use as a benchmark for assessing the kind of world we'd like to see come about. There's little doubt that the current world order doesn't meet this criterion: it surely can't be said that social and economic inequalities in the real world are arranged so as to benefit the least advantaged in the global economy. So if we want to commit to some kind of Rawlsian account of global justice, then we will have to take seriously a commitment to transfer resources from the rich world to the poor, and to enhance the system of global governance to widen the provision of basic liberties.

## COMPASSION

Although such a position leaves plenty of specifics to be settled, we at least now have a couple of resources to help us decide, in the broadest sense, what kinds of actions are the right ones: they ought to be compatible with the demands of global justice, and also ought to maximize well-being to the extent that it's possible to judge it sensibly. In practice, it may be that those two goals come into conflict. However, neither requirement seems dispensable to me, and so any sophisticated response to ethical issues such as global poverty will need to find some way to reconcile the two of them.

In the meantime, it may be that the discussion so far has struck you as leaving something very important out. In everyday life we often think about ethical concerns as somehow involving an emotional, or subjective, content. Even though we've moved away from the most abstract level of ethical thinking introduced earlier, we're still dealing with our ethical questions in a rational, even detached, way. In Rawls' account of justice, a lot rests on essentially self-centred reasoning – we wouldn't want to put *ourselves* in a situation where we might end up being disadvantaged (even if this aversion is purely hypothetical). In the case of utilitarianism, the calculations are explicitly impersonal ones – given a clever enough algorithm, even a computer would be able to perform 'good' actions.[19] What's missing here, it seems to me, is the rather difficult notion we brought up at the start of our discussion, the idea of a 'good will'. I noted then that any good moral reasoning would have to somehow exemplify this if it were to be truly persuasive, so we need to turn to it now and try to give the idea some content.

Even more so than the other concepts we've discussed, it's extremely hard to come up with an account of a good will that won't immediately be rejected as being, on the one hand, too partial, or, on the other, uselessly vague. This difficulty is to be expected – if the idea of a good will had been entirely settled, then there wouldn't be substantive ethical disagreements about it (beyond matters of simple resource allocation), and the whole field of moral philosophy would be otiose and complete. With this in mind, in what remains of this chapter, I sketch out one way of looking at the issue which may prove helpful. I don't believe for a minute that it will convince everyone, nor that it's rigorous enough to deserve to. However, it may provide an antidote to some of the more abstract notions we've been discussing so far, and possibly strike you as capturing the most important sense of ethics as something we should value and cherish.

We'll start by considering a very different tradition of moral thinking from the ones we've already covered. Most modern ethical theory – such as utilitarianism – is concerned with telling us what kinds of *actions* we ought to be performing. We saw earlier, in our discussion of moral saints, that selflessness can lead to the counterintuitive outcome of a person behaving entirely ethically (according to a given theory) and yet leading a barren and unfulfilled life. What's absent in the case of the moral saint is an appropriate set of character virtues. Although she might be doing the 'right' thing, the proper set of *motivations* is missing: she's acting purely according to the dictates of some theory or other, and is blind to other considerations, such as what kind of life is best in general, and what qualities ought to be cultivated beyond simply sending all one's money to the poor. Awareness of this problem has led, in the last few decades, to an increase of interest in some very ancient ideas about moral issues, and the revival in academic philosophy of something called 'virtue ethics'.

This tradition finds its most influential statement in Aristotle's *Nichomachean Ethics*, a brilliant but difficult work of philosophy written during the fourth century BC. In the *Ethics*, Aristotle, rather than being concerned with right and wrong actions in themselves, is interested in what counts as the best kind of life to live. He uses the term *eudaimonia* to describe the supreme good that humans aim for. There's no ready translation for this word in English (the closest to a literal rendition would be 'sweet angel'), but the notion has been variously described as the best kind of happiness we can attain, or the result of a life lived excellently. Aristotle considers the question of how we can 'live excellently': what kinds of concerns we ought to have, and how we should act on them.

His answer is that the ideal life is one that embodies the right set of virtues. 'Virtue' is quite an old-fashioned term in non-academic language, but can be understood here as referring to general character traits, or dispositions to feel a certain way in certain circumstances. So, instead of worrying too much about an impersonal procedure which renders certain actions 'right' and 'wrong', we instead ought to strive to cultivate the ideal set of personal qualities (bravery, responsibility, loyalty, and so on). When we're then confronted with difficult moral choices, we'll be able to deal with them in the appropriate way. In Aristotle's terms, the right virtues are those that enable us to do things 'at the right times, with reference to the right objects, towards the right people, with the right motive, and in the right way'.[20]

This kind of approach may well strike you as being a more 'human' way of looking at ethics than the others we've discussed. The attraction of Aristotle's theory is that it is an attempt to deal with our desires and emotions – the irreducibly subjective side of our engagement with the world. As you'll no doubt have noticed, though, it leaves some very important questions open: Just what are the 'right' virtues? Is it better to be a brave person (even though that can lead to foolhardiness) or a reserved one (even though that can lead to inaction when action is warranted)? And even if we do have the right set of virtues, how will that help us make difficult moral choices, such as deciding on the most effective way to distribute aid to the poor?

Aristotle does provide some answers to these obvious objections, such as the celebrated idea of the 'doctrine of the mean', in which he advocates those virtues lying between the extremes of behaviour. For critics of virtue ethics, however, the principal weakness of the theory is that it still doesn't with any clarity tell you what you *ought* to do – it simply suggests that individuals ought to have the right set of virtues, and then leaves it frustratingly vague what they actually are.[21] In what follows here, I don't intend to confront those arguments head on – the issues are complex, and by no means resolved in current academic debate.[22] Instead, I'll take one particular virtue – compassion – and argue that no account of the morality of global poverty can afford to ignore it. I suggest that it's the quality of compassion – the capacity we have as human beings to empathize with the plight of others – that gives us one good way of understanding what a 'good will' is with regard to moral deliberation on the situation of the world's poorest.

One philosopher who took the idea of compassion very seriously was Rousseau, the same writer who inspired Rawls' idea of a hypothetical contract. Rousseau had an intriguing view of human nature. He's famous for his notion of the 'noble savage' – the idea that the human spirit is often oppressed and constrained by the baggage of complex modern society. In Rousseau's philosophy, material progress (including in the arts or the sciences) tends to inflame our innate sense of self-importance, and with it our desire for status and recognition. This has the effect of generating unequal, hierarchical communities where the needs of those at the bottom of the ladder are given little attention and the desires of those at the top are privileged. By contrast, pre-industrial societies, including the simplest hunter-gatherer communities, allow a less distorted type of psychology to flourish. According to Rousseau, the absence of many of the trappings of modern life, such as clearly defined ranks and the economics of interdependence, makes it easier for individuals to maintain a less destructive mode of engagement with one another. Accordingly, his political philosophy strives to recreate a situation where individual competitive drives are subsumed within a more cooperative model, and certain conditions obtaining in the so-called 'state of nature' are recreated.

We don't need to concern ourselves here with Rousseau's theories of government or the plausibility of his claims about pre-civilized psychology.[23] What's more interesting is his view of what the most fundamental drives governing our behaviour in the pre-civilized world are. He doesn't think that self-interest is the most pressing of these, even when resources are scarce and competition might be expected. On the contrary, it is compassion, or pity, that provides the impetus for our engagement with other people. Rousseau has a very optimistic picture of human nature. We take an active pleasure, he thinks, in helping others, and are made unhappy when we're unable to prevent the suffering of those we come into contact with. This a 'pre-rational' response to the world around us, and doesn't require anything like a complex moral code to find purchase. In Rousseau's view, humans are naturally compassionate creatures – it's only the imposition of badly ordered societies and rules that allow other, less beneficent, drives to take over.

In fact, the exercise of compassion is so important to our development as persons in Rousseau's account, that we can't be said to have any real moral sense without it. Put simply, compassion is the activity of placing oneself in the position of another, of feeling another's suffering as one's own. Unless we are able, at some level, to do this, then morality as an institution doesn't make much sense. As Rousseau writes in *Emile*, his book on the ideal education of a young man,

> So long as [Emile's] sensibility remains limited to his own individuality, there is nothing moral in his actions. It is only when it begins to extend outside of himself that it takes on, first, the sentiments and, then, the notions of good and evil which truly constitute him as a man.[24]

Rousseau says later in the same work that 'the entire right of nature is only a chimera if it is not founded in a natural need of the human heart.'[25] Compassion, therefore, is not a state that can be adopted or rejected on a whim – it is the impulse that makes the whole of morality explicable. This is similar to Williams' point about the amoralist. Without our ability to 'feel alongside' those who are suffering, the edifice of moral thought and law (the 'right of nature') is just a chimera – an illusion.

This way of expressing the origins of morality is, I think, a useful antidote to some of the more technical treatments we've been considering thus far. When we reflect on the massive inequality that currently blights the world – the huge disparities in wealth, and the crushing hardships that affect so many people across the planet – surely the correct response (in Aristotle's sense of feeling the 'right' thing) is compassion. As human beings, we ought to be sensitive to the sufferings of others, and to feel sympathy with their situation as a matter of instinct, not theory. This isn't a licence for condescension, the kind of paternalistic pity that someone in a superior position might feel towards one at a lower rank in life. Instead, it's the action of 'feeling alongside', the imaginative act of putting oneself in the place of another. The result of this is to feel a fraction of the pain and suffering that those in the real world experience in a much more tangible and profound sense. Only by making this imaginative leap can we hope to be motivated in the truest ethical sense. If we're truly incapable of feeling the pain of others in this way, then it's legitimate to cast doubt over whether our actions have any genuine moral content, however much good or bad may result from them in other ways.

Compassion, then, seems to me to be an essential part of any ethical response to the desperate situation of the world's poor. To remain unmoved by the scale of human suffering implies, I think, the lack of this essential component of our humanity. In a very small way, I have been exposed to some of the consequences of extreme poverty first-hand. Coming face to face with chronic deprivation is a sobering and upsetting experience. Wanting to *do* something about it is natural, and the challenge such suffering poses to our normal way of living and working is profound. That doesn't mean that one has to drop everything and devote every second of one's life to helping the poor (as the crudest reading of Singer's position implies); it does, however, present us with the imperative of finding out more, looking into the issues, and weighing up how much we, as individuals, could help alter the situation.

## FROM THEORY TO ACTION

You may well be feeling that the various debates and difficulties we've covered have made your thinking about the ethics of aid more confused than it was at the start. One of the real difficulties of thinking about such issues is that there *is* no settled consensus on what the best approach is, despite what the more strident advocates of a certain philosophy would have you believe. I've not tried to hide that, or to pretend that there are simple solutions where there aren't any. To recap, though, these are the key conclusions from this chapter and the previous one:

- Philosophical approaches to ethical issues involve enquiry into the rational basis of our ideas. If we can't justify our beliefs according to a reasonably impartial set of considerations, then they're beliefs we may have to reject.

- There are good reasons for rejecting the idea that amorality is a serious lifestyle choice, that people outside our immediate community somehow fail to merit moral concern, and that our failure to act has any less moral significance than our actions. We do have responsibilities to people in distant geographical locations and from different cultures. It is, however, legitimate and reasonable to place those responsibilities in context, and to balance our obligations to aid the poorest in the world with the obligations we have to ourselves and those closest to us.

- Any action taken to address the plight of the global poor will have to take into account a range of considerations. Three of the most important, as argued here, are (a) that the consequences of our actions promote the most utility; (b) that this is compatible with a reasonable definition of justice; and (c) that our actions are driven by a genuine sense of compassion for others.

# 4  Giving

We've spent considerable time looking at the origins of world economic inequality and considering ethical questions in the abstract. It's time we put the two together. In this chapter, we'll cover one of the two main ways of addressing poverty: the donation of money, time, or some other service, from rich countries to poor ones. This is not the only means by which a country or community could conceivably escape poverty. Indeed, as we'll see, it's debatable whether *any* country has lifted itself out of poverty purely as a result of aid. However, it's certainly the more high-profile of the two methods of addressing global imbalances, the other being reform of international trade, and so we'll look at how the aid agencies operate, the criticisms of them from various sources, and the arguments in their favour. At the end of the chapter, I assess how successful they've been and whether we should support them, taking into account the broad ethical concerns we've just outlined.


## THE AGENTS OF VIRTUE

In the following passage from *Framley Parsonage*, the Victorian novelist Anthony Trollope satirizes the efforts of missionary societies, the 'aid agencies' of the time. The fictional exchange takes place prior to a lecture given by Mr Harold Smith on the islanders of Borneo and various attempts to improve them. His interlocutor is Mr Supplehouse, a cynic in the mould of Glaucon, who has a healthy scepticism of such endeavours:

'And how do you intend to begin with them?' asked Mr Supplehouse, the business of whose life it had been to suggest difficulties.

'Begin with them – oh – why – it's very easy to begin with them. The difficulty is to go on with them, after the money is all spent. We'll begin by explaining to them the benefits of civilisation.'

'Capital plan!' said Mr Supplehouse. 'But how do you set about it, Smith?'

'How do we set about it? How did we set about it with Australia and America? It is very easy to criticise; but in such matters the great thing is to put one's shoulder to the wheel.'

'We sent our felons to Australia,' said Supplehouse, 'and they began the work for us. And as to America, we exterminated the people instead of civilising them.'

'We did not exterminate the inhabitants of India,' said Harold Smith, angrily.

'Nor have we attempted to Christianise them, as the bishop so properly wishes to do with your islanders.'

'Supplehouse, you are not fair,' said Mr Sowerby, 'neither to Harold Smith nor to us; – you are making him rehearse his lecture, which is bad for him; and making us hear the rehearsal, which is bad for us.'

'Supplehouse belongs to a clique which monopolises the wisdom of England,' said Harold Smith, 'or, at any rate, thinks that it does. But the worst of them is that they are given to talk leading articles.'

'Better that, than talk articles which are not leading,' said Mr Supplehouse. 'Some first-class official men do that.'[1]

Trollope is, of course, a master observer of minor human frailties. This extract might as well have been written in the present, so astutely does it capture the weaknesses of both the supporters and detractors of the aid effort. On the one hand, Mr Smith exhibits the sentiment which has been so fatal to so many development projects: 'It is very easy to criticize; but in such matters the great thing is to put one's shoulder to the wheel.' There is a blithe assumption that, if the intentions are good enough, then *any* intervention is liable to do some good. The details can be sorted out, and criticisms dealt with, later. Mr Smith also displays the condescension and self-confidence so common among celebrity aid endorsers: 'Begin with them – oh – why – it's very easy to begin with them.'

But Mr Smith's tormentor, Supplehouse, comes off just as badly. The best line in the exchange is Mr Smith's barb that his critics are 'given to talk leading articles'. Plenty of clever people have taken potshots at aid industry efforts, often with considerable ignorance of how things work. That's why Bob Geldof, who has attracted a fair bit of criticism in his time, gets so cross: 'I am withering in my scorn for the columnists who say, "It's not going to work,"' he said in a newspaper interview. 'Even if it doesn't work, what do they propose? Every night forever watching people live on TV dying on our screens?'[2] Showing up foolishness and naivety is very much easier than attempting to do something that will have an impact on the problems. When we try and make sense of the various efforts underway to alleviate poverty, we should retain Mr Smith's enthusiasm for the possibility of improvement, modified by Mr Supplehouse's intolerance for woolly expression and imprecise aims. As we'll see, there is no shortage of criticisms of the aid agencies working today; some are valid, some less so.

One of the problems, though, in engaging with the aid industry is that it comprises so many groups and organizations, all with different emphases, cultures, policies and scopes. At the top of the pile are the massive international bodies, such as the UN Development Programme, the World Bank and the World Food Programme. These all do different things, but are similar in one respect: they're huge bureaucracies, with offices all over the world and staffs of thousands. Their budgets are equally huge: the World Food Programme had a projected budget of $6.7 billion in 2009, while the UN Development Programme was able to draw on $828 million for 2010–2011.[3]

Slightly smaller in size, but still at the big end of the spectrum, are the aid agencies of various rich world governments, such as United States Agency for International Development (USAID); Department for International Development (DFID) in the UK; the European Commission; *Deutsche Gesellschaft für Technische Zusammenarbeit* (GTZ), one of several German aid agencies, and so on. The aims and strategies of these organizations vary tremendously. Some, like many of the US agencies, operate in concert with national foreign policy. Others, like DFID, don't. Some are government departments proper, others are executive agencies. The key similarity, however, is that they are charged with disbursing money collected from the taxpayers of their respective countries. They are public bodies and distribute public funds.

Next on the list are the big international charities, such as Oxfam, Catholic Overseas Development (CAFOD) and Save the Children. These bodies prefer to call themselves 'NGOs' (nongovernmental organizations), but we don't have to adopt such pointless acronymization. Like the international and national aid agencies, the big charities operate large bureaucracies and have presences in many countries around the world. They may take a general interest in poverty (like Oxfam) or specialize in one aspect of development, such as child welfare (like Save the Children). Unlike the national bodies, they don't principally draw on public funds, but raise money from other sources. This may involve direct appeals to the public, solicitation of bequests, operation of retail and other commercial operations, corporate fundraising, or whatever other methods their marketing departments can come up with. It's also possible for charities to receive public money directly, via government grants, or indirectly, such as in the fees they collect for their consultancy services or for implementing a particular project. None of the big charities would be happy to be aligned with a particular political point of view, though in practice, they certainly do take positions on political issues: some (perhaps

most) lobby actively for generally left-of-centre economic policies, while others are keener on free-market approaches.

Finally, there are the smaller charities, such as individual trust
funds and organizations working in a single small region. These
might be relatively well-endowed, or they may be literally a one-
man or one-woman band. They might be headed up by a wealthy
patron from the West or run by a national of the country in which
they operate. They may have access to secure funding, perhaps
from a large bequest or corporate sponsorship, or exist hand-to-
mouth, always seeking fresh support from different sources.
Some charities are set up by individuals who've volunteered on
development projects in the past, and there are a plethora of
church groups and small corporate philanthropic bodies. Some
focus on poverty alleviation, some on lobbying, and some on
civil rights work. Small bodies often maintain themselves by taking on work for bigger charities, taking advantage of their size
and knowledge of local conditions to deliver some service better than the large organization is able to do (such as writing a
report on an aspect of poverty reduction, or distributing
resources through a well-established network). The smaller
charities tend to have very specialized aims, such as running a
single orphanage or promoting wildlife diversity in a particular
region.

The huge differences between a behemoth like the UN Development Programme and a tiny charity promoting sustainable
fishing in Lake Victoria, for example, makes it difficult to draw
exact comparisons between them. I haven't even mentioned the
competing priorities of religious and secular organisations; the
benevolent arms of political parties, trade unions and multinational corporations; or the occasional outburst of giving occa-
sioned by celebrity appeals such as Live Aid. In essence, though,
all aid agencies and efforts are involved in the same thing: trans-
ferring capital (money, goods, time or skills) from rich people
(mostly, though not exclusively, in the rich world) to poor ones. All
of them, broadly speaking, want to see poor countries replicate

the economic prosperity of the rich ones, or at least to ameliorate some of the worst effects of extreme poverty.[4]

You might therefore think that such organizations would be popular in the countries where they work. In some cases, they are. Well-run organizations delivering essential services are very popular. But it's surprising the degree to which the aid industry, in all its forms, attracts disapproval. The title of this section, for example, comes from a travel memoir called *Dark Star Safari* by Paul Theroux. As he passes through the Great Rift Valley in East Africa, Theroux grows increasingly impatient with the attitude and actions of the aid workers he comes across. Very soon, he begins to see them as part of the problem, not the solution:

> There were many vehicles in Mzuzu, the most expensive of them of course were the white four-wheel drives displaying the doorside logos of charities, every one that I had ever heard of and some new ones – People to People, Mission Against Ignorance and Poverty, The Food Project, Action Aid, Poverty Crusade, and more. [. . .] There were more charities in Malawi than ever. Charities and agents of virtue and NGOs were now part of the Malawi economy, certainly one of the larger parts. The charities in Malawi were troughs into which most people were unsuccessfully trying to insert their snouts. [. . .] I began to understand the futility of charity in Africa. It was generally fuelled by the best motives, but its worst aspect was that it was non-inspirational. Aliens had been helping for so long and were so deeply entrenched that Africans lost interest – if indeed they had ever had it – in doing the same sort of work themselves.[5]

Is Theroux right? Have the actions of aid agencies actually made things *worse* for poor countries?

This question cuts right to the heart of current debates about aid. And, as I mentioned in the Introduction, positions on this issue tend to be firmly entrenched. In what follows I'll try to take a balanced view, looking first at arguments for the efficacy of aid and following with those against. I won't try to hide my own views, but I will try to keep them in the background. At the end of the chapter, you should be in a position to assess whether 'giving' adequately meets the demands of compassion and justice that we discussed earlier. If it does, then you have a moral obligation to get involved and help out. If it doesn't, then you might want to look for other ways of addressing the problem of global inequality.

## BREAKING THE POVERTY TRAP

As we saw in the first chapter, many of Africa's problems have their roots in circumstances that are hardly the 'fault' of its inhabitants. Environmental factors conspired to make indigenous development difficult, and the legacy of colonialism and exploitation did nothing to improve the situation. As a result, according to some writers on international development, Africa has ended up stuck in a 'poverty trap'. Its low economic starting point, coupled with artificial disadvantages imported from overseas, mean that it stands no chance of working its own way out of deprivation. What is needed, it's argued, is a radical increase in the amount of aid sent from the rich world. Only with the injection of mammoth sums of money can the conditions of the poverty trap be broken and a sustainable push towards growth triggered.

One of the key advocates of this approach is the former special adviser to the UN Secretary General, Jeffrey Sachs. In 2005, his book *The End of Poverty* was a major driving force behind the Live 8 and Make Poverty History campaigns. The book attracted the support of celebrities, such as Bono, as well as 'serious' politicians like Britain's Tony Blair. Sachs is possibly the most influential advocate of aid as the principal tool to reduce worldwide economic inequality, so we should take careful note of his arguments.

Sachs' key idea is that once the level of capital within a society falls below a certain level, it's impossible to replace it indigenously. What he means by capital is quite wide-ranging; it includes financial resources, human capital (such as skills), industrial capital (such as roads, machines and communications) and environmental capital (productive land, fertile soils, empty land to exploit, and so on). When resources in a poor country reach a critically low level, Sachs believes, they're destined to keep falling or, at least, to flat-line indefinitely. This is because individuals become so pushed just to make ends meet – to find enough to eat, to clothe them-selves and their families – that they have no left-over resources to invest for the future. Because they have no 'stores' of capital, each natural disaster or structural pressure (such as population growth) has a disproportionate impact. Poor countries do not have the wherewithal to absorb the shock, and so the capital problem gets ever worse. Over the long term, this vicious circle leads to abso-lute poverty, such as what we see today in many parts of Africa.

Because, in Sachs' view, the problem is essentially one of resources, the only solution is a large injection of capital from out-side. The level of capital circulating in the economy needs to be raised to a point where the constant drain on resources caused by population growth, disease and natural disaster is outweighed by the productive investment within the system. Households need to have sufficient resources to pay taxes and invest for the future, enabling government to invest in more forms of capital creation, thereby generating the economic growth necessary to offset the wearing effects inherent in any economy:

> Foreign help, in the form of official development assistance (ODA), helps to jump-start the process of capital accumulation, economic growth, and rising household incomes. [. . .] Growth becomes self-sustaining through household savings and public investments supported by taxation of households. In this sense, foreign assistance is not a welfare handout, but is actually an investment that breaks the poverty trap once and for all.[6]

Current levels of development assistance have been insufficient to trigger this process, according to Sachs. Although aid has been flowing to Africa and other poor regions for over fifty years, the sums have not been large enough to generate the step change required to break the poverty trap. The size of aid flows isn't the only important thing – the timing of aid is too. Sachs thinks the surge should be delivered as quickly as possible, and that a large volume of aid distributed over ten years is not as valuable as the same amount allocated in one year.

What reasons do we have for thinking that Sachs might be right? Certainly, there's much intuitive plausibility about the scenario he sketches. Imagine trying to live on less than 65 cents a day, as half of Africa's population are forced to do. That 65 cents has to support not just you but, in all likelihood, a large family. Almost all of it will have to go for food. Even more likely, precious time would be spent growing food in order to supplement the food you buy, making it impossible to pursue an alternative, more productive career. Any medical emergency would further erode what few resources you have. And, even if it proved possible to survive on such a paltry income, it would certainly not be possible to save money for the future, or to invest in better means of generating resources. And if there is a natural catastrophe, such as a drought or famine, then any progress you had made would be wiped out or reversed. The only way out of this vicious circle, if Sachs is right, is for someone to inject capital from outside. It's no good expecting the Africans themselves to create the conditions for growth: most of them are too busy trying to survive.

A second reason for thinking Sachs is right is that many of Africa's problems are in fact a result of the continent's environment, rather than some intrinsic feature of the populace. As we saw when we looked at Jared Diamond's account of economic development, Africa is a particularly difficult place to make a good living. There are significant structural problems, such as the lack of indigenous large domestic animals. Some of these have been remedied over time – there are plenty of cows and horses in Africa now – but some have not. There are still geographical issues: many African countries have no ready access to the sea, and thus find the cost of trade ruinously high. Most important of all is the presence of widespread epidemic disease. Sachs makes much of this, arguing that malaria and AIDS are not just significant consequences of poverty but also

causes of it. Even rich-world governments struggle to make investments in environments subject to chronic disease. The construction of the Panama Canal, for instance, was delayed for over thirty
years because of the malaria and yellow fever that afflicted the
workers and it was only after an expensive programme of disease
eradication was undertaken that work was able to continue.[7]

The important thing about these diseases is that they can be
treated. There are very good treatment programmes for malaria,
and increasingly good ones for HIV and AIDS. If the presence of
these diseases is a significant element of the poverty trap, and we
have the means to remove it, then surely a concerted effort on the
part of the West is the answer. In 2001, Sachs chaired a committee
of economists that produced an influential report arguing that poor
health is a major cause of poverty, and that aid spending should be
raised from $6 billion (the level then) to $27 billion a year. This would
mean the principal culprits of poor health and premature death in
Africa (malaria, tuberculosis, AIDS, diarrhoea and maternal mortal-
ity) could be removed from the picture. If $27 billion sounds like a
lot, it's worth placing this number in the context of the $25 *trillion*
generated by the rich-world economies annually.[8]

For the proponents of increased aid, these points are compelling.
After all, it's not the Africans' *fault* that they suffer disproportion-
ately from such virulent diseases, and the fact that they are saddled
with them is a major reason they've remained poor (not to mention
the staggering degree of human suffering that has been caused).
Given the low level of capital in African economies, there's no hope
of generating the resources to combat the problem indigenously.
On the other hand, the money and expertise do exist in the rich
world, so the right thing to do, morally speaking, is to transfer them.
The incentive of compassion and the demands of justice make this
a policy that any reasonable person would support. And the figures
Sachs proposes – a thousandth of the world's annual income for the
sake of disease eradication – make sense on utilitarian lines too.

Sachs' case is bolstered by similar successful interventions of the
past. Smallpox has been eradicated by concerted international

action, and there continues to be progress made against polio and other diseases. Perhaps the most famous example of large-scale international aid, though, is the Marshall Plan, a series of huge loans and grants made by the United States to the countries of Western Europe. Devastated by the Second World War, the economies of Europe's democracies were in poor shape. The fragility of their manufacturing base, coupled with the daunting costs of reconstruction, made it seem unlikely that they would be able to claw their way back to prosperity unaided. In their own way, they were at risk of falling into a poverty trap: falling incomes and a dearth of ready capital presented the spectre of a vicious circle of decline. The tinderbox of ideological conflict was ever present, something that is also the case in contemporary Africa. In the immediate post-war period, George Marshall, the US Secretary of State, put his name to an assistance programme which got Europe back on its feet. Huge sums of money – more, as a share of GDP, than the US currently devotes to overseas aid today – were pumped into the flagging capitalist economies of Europe, prompting a period of sustained growth and prosperity which still underpins their buoyant economies.[9]

The Marshall Plan was not, of course, an act of unalloyed altruism. The Americans were mindful of the march of communism and of the danger to their own interests of an impoverished and fractious Europe. Still, what Churchill is alleged to have called 'the most unsordid act in history'[10] was exactly that: a policy of enlightened self-interest that worked for the common good. The parallel with the international aid situation is close: it's not in the interests of the rich world to see the poor world slide further into deprivation. The results would be increased instability, migration, and the fostering of international terrorism.

But there was an important difference between the Marshall Plan and Sachs' proposals. United States intervention in Europe was concerned with propping up developed economies, not societies with no history of industrialization. The Americans were able to work with established companies to revive economies that had already proved their potential. Sachs, by contrast, proposes pumping money into economies that have never enjoyed any level of success, and his policies are more concened with social protection than growth. Nonetheless, the broad intention of both programmes is the same – to break the jaws of the poverty trap with a huge injection of capital targeted at strategic sectors. Just as an application of capital proved capable of reinvigorating the moribund economies of post-war Europe, so the mobilization of the rich world's resources could transform the prospects of African economies, according to proponents of the Sachs approach.

## THE DEVELOPMENT PLAN

The original Marshall Plan had specific goals. If a similar project were launched today to help the poorest break out of the poverty trap, what would its benchmarks for success be? How would the money be raised, and how would it be spent? As we saw in Chapter 2, decisions about the allocation of resources are among the hardest to make. Even if we believe that large-scale aid is a good thing, dividing the cake up between the various competing priorities is a daunting challenge.

One very ambitious attempt to direct the entirety of the world's development efforts also comes from Jeffrey Sachs' leadership. In 2002, the UN Millennium Project, which Sachs headed, was asked by the UN Secretary General to advise on how best to coordinate the international aid effort. He and his team worked on a series of policies to achieve the so-called Millennium Development Goals (MDGs), which comprise an important statement of what the aid community thinks should be done by 2015. Unlike many other statements of intent, the MDGs are precise, and they are time bound. The whole of the UN system, as well as every national agency whose government has signed the Millennium Declaration, are committed to these goals. Many charities share the aspiration to achieve them and have lobbied national governments to fund progress towards them. They're such an important part of the aid industry's activities – its joint 'mission statement', if you will – that they're worth reproducing (almost) in full here. The goals are divided into 'targets', each bearing down on a specific part of the development problem.[11]

| Goal | Target |
|---|---|
| 1. Eradicate extreme poverty and hunger | 1. Halve, between 1990 and 2015, the proportion of people whose income is less than one dollar a day<br>2. Halve, between 1990 and 2015, the proportion of people who suffer from hunger |
| 2. Achieve universal primary education | Ensure that by 2015 children everywhere, boys and girls alike, will be able to complete a full course of primary schooling |
| 3. Promote gender equality and empower women | Eliminate gender disparity in primary and secondary education, preferably by 2005, and to all levels of education no later than 2015 |
| 4. Reduce child mortality | Reduce by two-thirds, between 1990 and 2015, the under-five mortality rate |
| 5. Improve maternal health | Reduce by three quarters, between 1990 and 2015, the maternal mortality ratio |
| 6. Combat HIV/AIDS, malaria, and other diseases | 1. Have halted by 2015 and begun to reverse the spread of HIV/AIDS<br>2. Have halted by 2015 and begun to reverse the incidence of malaria and other major diseases |
| 7. Ensure environmental sustainability | 1. Integrate the principles of sustainable development into country policies and programs and reverse the loss of environmental resources<br>2. Halve by 2015 the proportion of people without sustainable access to safe drinking water and basic sanitation<br>3. By 2020 to have achieved a significant improvement in the lives of at least 100 million slum dwellers |

(There is an eighth goal, entitled 'Develop a global partnership for development', but this is slightly more diffuse than the others, and we'll take a look at some of the ideas associated with it in the following chapter.)

The MDG goals may remind you of the list of objectives for the Katine project. Aid agencies love producing such to-do lists. I've witnessed first-hand the extraordinary time and effort they devote to making sure that the wording of such documents is as good as it can be. The MDGs can be seen as the 'master list' of such goals, and all other compatible aid efforts in some sense derive their content from it.

As their name suggests, the MDGs were agreed in 2000. At the time of this writing, there are only five years left before they're due to be achieved. How far has Sachs' vision been realized in that time?

According to the UN's own 2009 report on progress, achievements have been mixed. The proportion of the populations in the developing world classified as living in extreme poverty fell slightly, and the numbers of children enrolled in primary education rose. There were also successes in the fight against infectious diseases, particularly measles. However, the bulk of the report's assessment is gloomy. The worldwide recession is predicted to have a significant effect on all the development goals – 64 million more people were expected to be living in extreme poverty by 2010, even without extra crises, such as natural disasters or wars. Rich countries, which generally commit to fixing aid budgets as a proportion of national income, will have less to contribute as their economies shrink. Poor countries will also suffer from the reduction in the scale of global trade, not least because of higher food prices. A look at the statistics in the report makes it clear that many of the goals will not be met by the 2015 deadline. Some targets, such as halving the proportion of people suffering from hunger, are more distant now than they were in 1990 (in sub-Saharan Africa).[12]

It is, of course, very difficult to obtain reliable statistics from some of the countries where aid money is being spent, so it's not entirely certain how well or badly each individual target is faring. And it's also true that the commitments made by rich-country governments are hard to keep track of – despite the extra money promised at such gatherings as the Gleneagles G8 meeting in 2005, for example, it's probably the case that contributions are still below the level Sachs would like to see. Nonetheless, it's sobering to note that after ten years of extraordinary international cooperation and agreement, a majority of the MDGs look unlikely to be achieved. Although a decade is a short time in the world of international economics, it does follow a half century of aid efforts, all of which have produced similarly disappointing results.[13]

What's the problem? Is it that the rich world is not committed enough? This is certainly possible. However, it's important to note that many economists don't agree with Sachs. They think that a step change in levels of aid won't have the effects he expects because large injections of cash into poor-country economies simply aren't guaranteed to work. As a result, the MDGs, and the methods advocated by Sachs to meet them, are doomed to failure. To see why, we need to look at some of the arguments against increases in aid spending.

## THE LORDS OF POVERTY

The basic charge against aid is simple to state. As we saw in the first chapter, since the establishment of the Bretton Woods institutions in the aftermath of the Second World War, some previously impoverished countries have leapt forward and joined the ranks of the developed world. India, China and much of Southeast Asia have lifted millions out of poverty and made great strides towards delivering a quality of life for their citizens on a par with that of the West. Africa, however, has remained stubbornly poor. In fact, in many respects most African countries are worse off now that they were when they gained independence in the 1950s and 1960s, and Africa is the only continent to have become poorer over the past 25 years.[14] It has also been the primary focus of the aid industry. Between 1970 and 1999, aid rose as a share of the GDP of African countries from 5 per cent to 17 per cent. During the same period, the rate of growth in those economies fell from 2 per cent to zero, or worse.[15]

The obvious conclusion to draw from this is that aid doesn't really do anything to improve the economic prospects of poor countries and may even make them worse. In his influential book, *The White Man's Burden*, William Easterly presents a critique of the belief that aid can transform poor countries into rich ones. He is a sharp critic of the Sachs approach, and his argument has two main strands: (a) there is no such thing as the 'poverty trap'; it's a misleading way of characterizing the challenges faced by poor countries; and (b) the responses of the large aid bureaucracies have generally been unhelpful – sometimes simply ineffective, sometimes actively harmful. Easterly shares Sachs' dismay at the condition of much of the world's population and is certainly not indifferent to their suffering. However, he disagrees that more aid is the answer to the problem (at least as currently delivered), and thinks that there needs to be a radical rethink of the nostrums of the development industry. To see why he holds this view, we'll look at his two claims in turn.

First, Easterly points out that, if you go back far enough (to 1950, rather than the 1980s), you see that the growth rates of the poorest countries were comparable then to those of the rest of the world. Which countries are the poorest also changes – eleven of the twenty-eight poorest countries in 1985 were not in the poorest fifth in 1950. It's only in relatively recent times that the poorest countries have suffered catastrophic failures of growth. Before that, even countries with very little capital seemed capable of generating economic growth. The lesson Easterly draws from this is that the 'trap' simply doesn't exist. Although there are no doubt impediments to growth from being poor, there is no automatic vicious circle which necessitates outside intervention.[16]

If the poverty trap isn't to blame, though, then why have poor countries (and African countries in particular) ended up in such a terrible state? Whereas Sachs points the finger at environmental considerations, such as widespread disease, Easterly thinks the answer is more often bad government. According to him, the most important factor in a country's prospects is the probity and competence of its administrators: poor countries actually achieve higher levels of growth than rich ones if their governments are democratic, accountable and reasonably well-run.[17] There are lots of ways that a government can be bad: it can be repressive and totalitarian, corrupt, or simply woefully incompetent. In each one of these cases, meaningful development will be impossible. Money will be wasted or stolen, and the virtuous circle that Sachs envisions, where household income feeds into taxation, which feeds into higher levels of investment, will never happen. For Easterly, the more important brake on a country's progress is supplied by poor government, not critically low levels of capital.

Easterly's claims are hotly contested. Just because rich countries are more often democratic, it doesn't necessarily follow that democracy has made them rich. There are important counter examples, such as China (which is certainly not democratic, though it's arguably very competently administered). The data on aid effectiveness are especially tricky to interpret. Whether a country does well or badly, picking the main reason for its performance is hard, and there are various academic studies that yield different accounts of how effective aid can be. However, there's certainly *doubt* over the claim that a large boost of foreign capital will trigger the step change in productivity that Sachs envisages. Easterly quotes an academic study by economists at the Center for Global Development which indicates that the more aid a country receives, the less effective that aid becomes. This is in itself unsurprising – most interventions, of any sort, produce less 'bang' for every extra 'buck', applied – but it does argue against the success of the 'big push' model of aid. Easterly claims that when a country's aid receipts exceed more than 8 per cent of its GDP, then the effect on its growth will actually be negative. He concludes:

> There is good data on public investment for twenty-two African countries over the 1970–1994 period. These countries' governments spent

$342 billion on public investment. The donors gave these same coun-
tries' governments $187 billion in aid over that period. Unfortunately,
the corresponding "step" increase in productivity, measured as production per person, was *zero*.[18]

What could possibly be going on here? How can the insertion
of outside investment into a poor economy result in a *fall* in
productivity?

We don't have to look very far to find examples of large-scale
government financial intervention having counterproductive
results. During the 1960s and 1970s, the vogue in Britain was for a
very interventionist government policy towards industry. Industrial growth was planned at the central level, and civil servants
worked hard to 'pick winners'. Many companies were publicly
owned. Others were given financial support if trading conditions
got difficult. Key industries, especially 'national champions', were
protected from the icy gales of the global marketplace. The results
were usually disastrous. Huge conglomerates, such as British Steel
and British Leyland, staggered from one disaster to another. The
cost to the taxpayer of propping up essentially uneconomic
entities continued to rise, even after the underlying viability of
the firms became highly questionable. Government intervention
in the companies, even when it was accompanied by large slices
of cash, was a key factor in the erosion of their competitiveness.
Freed from the onerous but necessary task of improving their own
internal processes in order to compete, they came to rely on government handouts. Though well-intentioned, the large-scale
planning of industrial policy, coupled with massive distribution of
taxpayer's cash, did nothing to improve the long-term profitabil-
ity of the companies in question. As a result, Britain, along with
most other capitalist economies, abandoned the 'top-down'
approach to industrial policy in the 1980s and 1990s, leading to a
sustained period of economic growth.

This example is, of course, contentious. There's plenty of debate
within the UK over whether the changes in government policy in

the 1980s were a good thing. After all, the Japanese and Korean economies in the 1970s were made competitive as a result of a very active programme of government ownership and intervention. As with the Marshall Plan, it's also open to question how similar the UK and African economies are, and whether lessons drawn in Europe have application to Africa. What such examples do demonstrate, though, is that spending large amounts of money doesn't *always* have good effects: there are at least some occasions where it can backfire and weaken an economy.

Easterly's argument runs along parallel lines. He's an opponent of a particular type of individual he calls 'the Planner'. The Planner is the epitome of the big-government bureaucrat, who, he claims, generally approaches problems with the attitude that they ought to be fixed with an ambitious, all-encompassing template for action. The Sachs approach to achieving the MDGs is an example of the Planner mentality – enormous energy went into drawing up a series of binding targets covering the full spectrum of aid challenges, to which large programmes of government money have been devoted. Planners take a technocratic approach to problems, trying to match financial inputs to expected outputs in a predictable, measurable way. We saw aspects of this in our discussion of utilitarianism and its limits – the attempt to use QALYs as a measure of health outcomes is a classic Planner strategy.

There are times, of course, when large-scale planning in government is a good and necessary thing. However, it can also end up being as ineffective as planned industrial policies were for British industry in the 1970s. In Easterly's view, there are three reasons large-scale aid efforts fail to come to grips with poverty.

First, Planners have a very mixed track record at creating economic growth, and if Planner-type policies failed to reliably create successful companies in the developed world, why would we expect them to do any better in the undeveloped world? Easterly believes that wealth is generated over the long term by the operation of markets, but also that it's difficult to *impose* successful markets where they don't exist indigenously. Wealth generation is a complex thing, involving millions upon millions of transactions and taking into account a range of deeply entrenched cultural values. A single blueprint for economic success is not something that can be worked out in an air-conditioned room in Washington DC and then simply exported to the rest of the world. The lesson of colonialism is that policies which work in one place (Europe) won't necessarily work elsewhere, at least without considerable modification and local input.

A good recent example is the 'structural adjustment loan', a key instrument used by the IMF in poor countries throughout the latter quarter of the twentieth century. These loans were advanced to poor countries on the condition that they would adjust their economies to resemble the open economies of the rich world: money was disbursed as long as public spending in the poor country was slashed, tariffs removed and government activities cut, often resulting in a reduction in public services, such as health care and education, and significant cuts in social security and welfare. These policies (arguably) are appropriate for rich-world countries with advanced economies, skilled work-forces and populations wealthy enough to weather the cuts. Their effect on the poor countries, however, was often disas-trous. Instead of fostering healthy private sectors, structural adjustment loans tended to create enormous suffering as essen-tial services were withdrawn, recipient governments were loaded with unpayable debts, and the standard of governance failed to improve at all.

Critics of Easterly's argument reject this claim. It's true, they say, that the Planners have failed to create prosperity in many places, but at the same time, they have succeeded in others. South Korea, for example, had almost fifteen years of incredible growth which was largely down to state planning. In addition, there is even con-tention over the effects of structural adjustment loans: some countries, such as Ghana, are believed to have derived at least some benefits from them. Just as Sachs is accused of overlooking the objections to his model of the 'big push', Easterly is accused by his critics of ignoring the evidence of successful Planner policies in other parts of the world.

The second reason Planners fail, according to Easterly, is that they're not directly accountable for their actions. If the owner of a company making widgets fails to create the product people really want to buy, then a competitor will step in to fill the gap and the company will go bust. The market provides a powerful *feedback* mechanism that holds the company directly to account for what it does. Accountability can work in other ways, too – a local politician can be voted out of office for failing to live up to a campaign promise. Aid Planners, on the other hand, are rarely held accountable for their actions by those they're trying to help. The extreme complexity of planning aid interventions, coupled with the frequent rotation of staff in the aid agencies, means that no UN bureaucrat, for example, ever has to face the consequences of a policy going wrong. This means that lessons aren't learned, and failed approaches are tried over and over again.

To the extent that Planners have any accountability at all, it's to the people that pay their salaries – the taxpayers of the rich world. The latter may have strong ideas about aid and want to see their money spent on certain things. So, for example, there may be pressure on aid workers to prioritize things that play well to a 'home' audience, whether or not such policies are wanted by the recipient country or have the best chance of succeeding. It's very rare to hear people in rich countries press for development of the private sector in poor countries, as it's often difficult to understand how this might help the poor (although it would). They are much happier supporting projects like hospital construction and road building, even though these often have a bad track record in supporting poverty reduction.[19]

## THE CORRUPTION PROBLEM

Third, Planners can be very bad at dealing with real-world problems that fail to mesh with their technocratic approach. The classic example is corruption. Planner models generally make few assumptions about human nature. Where such assumptions are made, they're generally benign ones. So it is that Sachs' model of capital production assumes that, when households have access to greater resources, they will begin to pay taxes, and that, when government has access to tax revenue, it will use it for public investment. Anyone who has lived in Africa knows that this is a pretty optimistic picture. Corruption is endemic in African countries, just as it once was in seventeenth-century Europe, and this is a significant drag on wealth creation.

Talking about corruption in Africa can lead one quickly to two unfair generalizations. The first is to give the impression that Africans are somehow 'intrinsically' more corrupt than, say, Europeans. I don't believe this to be the case at all, at least not in the sense that there is some racial or continent-wide lack of public morality. The second is to pretend that corruption doesn't exist in rich-world countries. This isn't the case either, though the economic impact of corruption in the rich world is, arguably, much less. However, there are features of corruption in Africa that make it extremely hard for Planner-type interventions to work well.

To start with, there are significant cultural differences between most Africans' expectations of the best way to distribute resources and those of the average European. Family and community ties are extremely strong in Africa, and there's a tendency to keep resources within an immediate circle. When it comes to perks, such as the decision-making power that comes with many government jobs or handouts, if an official in Kenya or Zambia doesn't use his power to advantage those close to him, then he's behaving in an unusual way. On a larger scale, this means that some African leaders make very little distinction between capital that is *theirs* to use and capital that belongs properly to the nation. As a result, government resources in some African countries are frequently used for the enrichment of the ruling elites. Sometimes, as in the case of Mobutu Sese Seko's kleptocracy in Zaire, the scale of this venality is staggering. In a country like Malawi, the sums of money involved might be much less but still enough to derail attempts to shore up the government's faltering budget.

Bad government is a real problem for large-scale aid interventions. There are almost too many examples of corruption ruining carefully thought-through aid projects to choose from. This one, from Paul Collier's book *The Bottom Billion*, is particularly striking:

> In 2004 a survey tracked money released by the Ministry of Finance in Chad intended for rural health clinics. The survey had the extremely modest purpose of finding out how much of the money actually reached the clinics – not whether the clinics spent it well, or whether the staff of the clinics knew what they were doing, just where the money went. Amazingly, less than 1 per cent of it reached the clinics – 99 per cent of it failed to reach its destination.[20]

When a staggering 99 per cent of donated resources are being diverted into the pockets of officials before they can reach their intended destination, it's not surprising that the effectiveness of aid is questioned. This is an extreme example, but plenty of other agencies have struggled to tackle corruption. Some organizations, particularly those with clout, such as the UN and the national agencies, have tried to get tough with corrupt regimes and tie future disbursements to reforms in governance. The problem with this approach is that those who would suffer from the withdrawal of aid – the poorest – are not the ones buying Mercedes Maybachs and putting their cash into Swiss bank accounts. So, as a rule, when the money runs out, the donors relent and keep propping things up. This avoids the awful spectacle of poor people dying as a result of the withdrawal of development funds, but it also does nothing to curb the excesses of their rulers. So the vicious circle continues (though, unlike Sachs' poverty trap, this one is entirely artificial).

Easterly's views on corruption have also been challenged. Just as his critics point out that there's no established *causal* link between democracy and prosperity, some commentators believe that there's also no necessary connection between corruption and poverty. Some countries seem to tolerate large levels of corruption with no adverse economic affects, while other, relatively 'clean' countries continue to suffer: China, for example, maintains business practices that would widely be considered corrupt in the West but continues to enjoy burgeoning economic success. The economist Mushtaq Khan has even argued that corruption, at least in some forms, can be beneficial for development.[21] It is difficult to see, though, how any intervention could achieve success in an environment such as Chad's, where so much of the intended cash goes missing. Whatever the ultimate effects on the economy, aid agencies are often guilty of handling corrupt administrations badly.

There are many other criticisms of the aid industry (it is, after all, easier to criticize than to suggest solutions), but I'll mention just two more here. The first is the charge that aid encourages a psychological dependence on Western intervention, and actually prevents home-grown development taking place. Such a phenomenon would be hard to measure quantitatively, since it's essentially a claim about people's attitudes and culture. An example may illustrate the point, though: during my short period working in Malawi, there was much discussion about opening a uranium mine in the north of the country. As a result of worries over the environmental and social impact of the project, consultation was undertaken with local people to determine whether the scheme should be allowed to go ahead. There were, of course, lots of reasons why the mine might have been a bad thing – it could have destroyed the local ecology, caused an influx of migrant workers, or created health problems. The interesting feedback from the review, however, was that many people were worried that it *would* be a success, and that as a result of the prosperity it would bring to the area, the aid they were currently entitled to (in the form of agricultural grants, mainly) would be jeopardized. In other words, the prospect of the region actually generating its own money was far less appealing than remaining subject to regular handouts.

This may seem like a rather mean-spirited example, a kind of throwback to the Victorian ethic where work is virtuous and charity is shameful.[22] Taken alone, it probably is – it would be entirely unsurprising if a vulnerable community were wary of new developments that could take away their one reliable means of staving off starvation. However, there is a worrying tendency for large-scale, year-on-year aid disbursements to create a deadening effect in the recipient countries, a weakening of indigenous capacities for enterprise and innovation. In heavily aid-dependent countries, the few young people able to take advantage of tertiary-level education are often quickly absorbed into the employ of the aid agencies on graduation, which usually pay far more than private businesses or government can. As a result, the problem of poor levels of ability within native institutions remains unaddressed. In countries where huge proportions of government spending comes from overseas agencies, which aren't accountable to the recipients of their activities, local people have less reason to engage in their own political processes, or take interest in what elected officials are doing.[23] And once aid becomes sufficiently embedded into the vital systems of a country, it can be hard to escape the negative effects.

This brings us to the last charge against the aid industry, that it has, in effect, assumed an imperialist role and taken over the business of running African countries from their own politicians. This is a charge that's made both by those on the political Left, critical of the power that institutions like the IMF and World Bank exercise over government spending, and those on the Right, who worry about the waste of resources being sent to corrupt regimes. In a sense, the aid agencies are damned if they do and damned if they don't: if they impose conditions on aid to prevent it being misused, then they're accused of being overbearing; if they don't, then they're seen as being too weak. The fact that it's the *aid agencies* that come in for criticism (rather than national governments in poor countries) is interesting, though. They're seen as the bodies with the power in the relationship, the ones who hold the key to the country's development. For both kinds of critics, Left and Right, aid agencies are guilty of acting like agents of the colonial past, albeit without acknowledging the similarities.

To be sure, there are some parallels between the old imperialists and the aid industry. Rich-country agencies have enormous power, simply because they hold the purse strings. In heavily aid-dependent countries, the very fact that outsiders provide such large proportions of government expenditure makes them extremely powerful. Moreover, some agencies, such as USAID, design their programmes with their own government's foreign policy goals in mind, and are therefore open to accusations that their programmes are part of a broader set of political objectives. Certainly, in the case of controversial instruments such as the structural adjustment loans, the aid industry has in the past been guilty of imposing solutions on poor countries, and taking an arrogant and high-handed approach to dealing with government interlocutors. Easterly worries about the return of colonialist values:

> Western intervention in the government of the Rest [the poor world], whether during colonization or decolonization, has been on the far side of unhelpful. The West should learn from its colonial history when it indulges neo-imperialist fantasies. They didn't work before and they won't work now.[24]

The accusation of neo-Imperialism brings us uncomfortably back to Paul Theroux's 'agents of virtue', gliding around in air-conditioned Land Cruisers, blithely signing off on unworkable projects, while having no accountability for them, and dictating policies to a supine and corrupt local government. This picture is very far from the generally optimistic one painted by Sachs and his supporters, but is it any more persuasive?

## SMALL IS BEAUTIFUL – OR PERHAPS NOT

Before we try to evaluate these competing claims, we need to take a step down from the heady world of the 'macro' aid projects, and consider smaller fry. Our discussion so far has focused almost exclusively on the biggest aid agencies. This isn't surprising, since they command the lion's share of resources and attention. However, as I noted at the beginning of the chapter, there are thousands of smaller charities and organizations working to combat poverty. Do these do any good, or are they irrelevant?

One of the advantages of smaller projects is that their effects can be seen sooner. A donation of £50 to an orphanage might have immediate results – the purchase of new materials, or the payment of workers' salaries for a period of time. With the massive agencies, such immediate results are much harder to track. Working with independent institutions also avoids the necessity of dealing directly with governments and officials, who in some countries (like Chad) may have little interest in seeing resources get to those who most need them.

Speaking personally, I can attest that it can be truly inspiring to see relatively small amounts of money achieve near-instant results. I can recall overseeing a disbursement of small amounts of cash (by UK standards) to the National Association of Business Women (NABW), which promotes business skills for Malawian women. The idea was simple – instructors would give intensive tuition in how to run basic income-generating activities, such as profit planning and keeping regular accounts. They would then support cooperatives of women with low-cost loans to set up village-based ventures, such as fish farming. Support and guidance would be given throughout the process, but the women would be expected to pay back the loans in due course out of the profits they made. The hope was that the businesses in the long run would be able to stand unaided, generating capital for the local economy just in the way Sachs outlines. The only difference was scale – the total budget for the entire scheme over several years was something like £20,000, meaning that individual projects ended up receiving tiny amounts of cash.

After the project had been a year or so in operation, I became part of an evaluation team. We visited several of the businesses set up by the women. The level of enthusiasm was infectious. In the middle of a terrible year for maize harvest, successful ventures, especially in small-scale farming, had been set up and were thriving. The small amounts of money involved were meticulously recorded and accounted for. Most importantly, the 'profit' columns in the handwritten ledgers were pretty healthy. After the loan instalments had been paid, there was enough left over to reinvest in the companies. Unlike in the case of simple handouts, there was a pride taken in the work done. Though the money had come from outsiders, the achievement was all local, from the Malawians who ran the charity to the women who actually made the money. It was hard not to feel that this was an ideal way to manage aid. At the very least, the scope for doing harm was limited, and the potential for doing good looked to be considerable.

The problem with this scenario, of course, is that it's very easy to be seduced by projects where one can see the immediate results, and even share some level of credit for them. There's still a question mark over whether such small-scale operations deliver worthwhile, *long-term* benefits. After all, initiatives such as this have been going on for a very long time, and it's not obvious that they contribute to the country-wide change in fortunes that aid visionaries, such as Sachs, would like to see.

It's notable, for instance, that national aid agencies, such as DFID and the European Commission, have in recent years tended to move away from project work such as this and concentrate instead on larger-scale initiatives. There is an emphasis on spending large blocs of money on so-called sector-wide approaches – targeting a country's entire health or education sectors, for example. Even more all-embracing are the moves towards general financial support, where aid agencies collaborate with one another to prop up the local government's overall spending budget and stay relatively hands-off in terms of how the money is allocated (that is, as long as the government has a credible plan to tackle poverty, is compliant with international human rights accords and is taking steps to improve its financial management and controls). There's also pressure on the agencies to contribute to regional schemes, which cut across many national programmes.

Why is the trend towards making aid projects larger and more comprehensive, when the attractions of small projects are so (superficially) obvious? One answer is that project work, as rewarding as it is to be involved in, is the way the aid industry has traditionally done things, and it hasn't worked. In the past, it was much more common for overseas development administrations to help build schools, clinics and roads. Within any given aid budget, there may have been countless small programmes going on, some of which might well have resembled the kind of work done by NABW. Over the decades since the Second World War, such work has had very little effect on the fortunes of the countries involved. There have been lots of buildings constructed in Zambia, and nurses trained in Mozambique, and roads laid in Nigeria, but the overall development picture has been relentlessly downward. Since the emphasis on projects had yielded so little, runs the argument, it's better to scale up the donations and work at a higher level. Rather than build clinics, why not reform the way the entire health sector operates; rather than work with small groups on income-generation, perhaps it would be better to help overhaul the entire structure of private-sector legislation and practice.

There are other reasons small projects are shunned by the big spenders of the aid world. One is simply a matter of practicality. It's exhausting and difficult to keep track of lots of different schemes, and the potential for money to go missing or to be wasted is high. This is something that the Katine project has found, and it has been one of the reasons for its waning popularity (at least with some of the commentators on the newspaper's website). Frankly, running any kind of project in Africa is a challenge, and the fewer the items that come under a single director's budget, the easier it is to monitor and assess their progress. One of the frequent criticisms made of aid agencies is that their administrative and staff costs are too high in proportion to their total spending. Running larger, broader schemes is one way of reducing the number of people involved in a particular area of spending.

More importantly, though, the move towards bigger programmes reflects a conscious decision on the part of donors to work with and through local governments whenever possible. This is in part an attempt to meet the criticism, noted above, that donors act like autonomous agents within African countries, undermining the relationship of accountability between the citizens and their political representatives. If aid money is exclusively delivered outside the normal channels of government, then the recipients will increasingly see government as irrelevant to their needs, and fail to take part in civic processes. In addition, if donors ignore the workings of government and fail to give officials funds with which to work, the government will never get better at delivering services. Although there are obvious risks in working closely with administrations that may be corrupt, and will almost certainly be bad at handling large flows of money, unless aid organizations get actively involved with local governments, it's unlikely that things will ever get better.[25]

As a result of this, public money from rich-world taxpayers is increasingly used for large-scale programmes, leaving the charitable sector to support individual projects. This can be a source of friction between more traditionally minded donors and those with a more contemporary approach. It also introduces a further level of complexity into discussions about whether aid is a 'good' or a 'bad' thing. Easterly, for example, generally has more time for smaller-scale work than he does for massive projects. He cites with approval a number of relatively modest schemes, such as a paramedic service in Bangladesh and a programme of AIDS awareness in India, which have clearly targeted aims and a limited focus. The advantage of fostering such projects, according to Easterly, is that they avoid the worst effects of the Planner mentality – they don't require huge bureaucracies, and they are responsive to the needs of local people in a way that sector-wide approaches can't be. The very lack of a utopian goal is their strength, and the fact that they involve people working at the grassroots level makes it more likely that the objectives will be ones that local people really want to see. The kind of development encouraged by such projects is more 'bottom-up' than 'top-down', and exhibits a mentality Easterly calls the Searcher. Connecting with individuals, rather than governments, increases the prospect of avoiding the worst aid industry mistakes.

Easterly's idea of the Searcher has been criticized too (as you'll not be surprised to hear). Supporters of big interventions, such as 'sector-wide approaches' (SWAPs), in which whole sectors of government activity such as education or health are supported *en bloc*, argue that they're actually more flexible than smaller charities, since funding decisions are taken by domestic officials as part of routine government business. Smaller charities may be forced to plan activities according to what they can deliver with their own limited pool of staff, rather than what's the best course of action for the recipient country. Because of this uncertainty over what works best, both kinds of development assistance are likely to continue alongside each other for the foreseeable future – government agencies will work with government agencies, and individuals with individuals.

It certainly adds another layer of choice for anyone interested in contributing. If you have a certain amount of money or time to donate, you might wonder whether you'd be better off supporting the large programmes aiming to achieve Sachs' step change in growth, or the little project devoted to installing clean water in a few villages. It's also possible, that after reading all the various claims and counterclaims above, that the whole business looks too flawed and complicated to bother with. Perhaps, despite all the good intentions we may have, we should simply throw up our hands and walk away.[26]

## ASSESSING AID

If the huge difference between the pro-aid and anti-aid arguments has left you feeling a bit nonplussed, you're not alone.
Debates over whether aid is a good, bad or indifferent thing are
currently very fierce. According to Graham Hancock, the author of
*Lords of Poverty*, a polemic against alleged corruption and incompetence in the aid industry,

> Development assistance is neither necessary nor sufficient for 'develop-
> ment': the poor thrive without it in some countries; in others, where it is
> plentifully available, they suffer the most abject miseries. Such suffering,
> furthermore, [. . .] often occurs not *in spite of* aid but *because* of it.[27]

Others, like Collier, are more circumspect:

> Aid does have serious problems, and more especially serious limita-
> tions. Alone it will not be sufficient to turn the societies of the bottom
> billion around. But it is part of the solution rather than the problem.
> The challenge is to complement it with other actions.[28]

And others still are very enthusiastic:

> In many countries, the conditions are now in place for a strong expan-
> sion of aid and assistance to make a powerful difference. Critics are no
> longer justified in making universal claims that aid to Africa is money
> wasted. Even in other countries – those that are not yet likely to use aid
> so effectively – we now know that outsiders can do a great deal to help
> create the preconditions for progress.[29]

In the face of such contradictory arguments, the temptation might
be to ignore the issue altogether, or at least not investigate it too
closely.

In what follows, while not attempting to give any definitive
answers, I suggest a few ways of thinking about the issue that
might help sort things out. First, let's recall some of the considerations we discussed when talking about the more abstract side of

ethical thought. The first is that it's not always possible to come up with views on complex phenomena (like the aid industry) which end up definitively proving that they are 'right' or 'wrong'. Unlike statements in science or logic, our ethical judgements are more a matter of doing the best we can with the information and the capability we have available to us. That might mean that we end up with a partial, vague or qualified position. That's not a failure of rationality, but rather an acknowledgement of the true difficulty of the question. Only a very unsophisticated thinker would conclude that *all* aid is good and ought to be supported, or that *all* aid is bad and ought to be outlawed, and none of the commentators we've discussed would subscribe to either of these extremes.

That doesn't make us powerless to make some value judgements, though. I suggested in Chapter 3 that we ought to have three broad considerations in mind when assessing the morality of aid: what a properly compassionate response would be to the problem of global inequality; what justice demands; and what kinds of policies are likely to have the best consequences.

It certainly seems to me that a person displaying a genuine virtue of compassion would want to see aid work of some kind continuing to have a real impact in the world. Whatever their weaknesses, aid agencies have been successful in combating the worst ravages of poverty in large parts of Africa. As the MDG report noted, aid agencies have made important progress against several infectious diseases, actions which have saved or improved the lives of millions of people. They've also been instrumental in the delivery of food aid to those that needed it during major famines and natural disasters, also saving uncountable lives. Without their actions, the short-term consequences of repeated environmental shocks would have been terrible. Even if there have been shortcomings in the modes of delivery of such aid, I find it hard to see that the alternative – letting people die when we have the tools to prevent it – has any appealing features at all. In the very long-term, such donations may have contributed to corruption, or have undermined the economic viability of the countries in question, and these are not negligible considerations. On balance, though, taking into account the proper exercise of compassion, the world in which aid agencies are active is far preferable to a hypothetical one in which they don't exist.

If we're genuinely concerned about justice, then there's also a powerful case to be made for the continued activity of the aid industry. As we've seen in our historical overview of the development of global inequality, it's impossible to separate the history of the rich world from that of the poor world. We in the West have benefited from positive environmental circumstances denied to large parts of the rest of the world. Where the rich world has interacted with the poor world, it has done so with a curious mix of benevolence, indifference and brutality. It would be profoundly unjust, in my view, not to seek to redress some of history's imbalances by sharing a proportion of the resources we've accumulated during that chequered past. Justice, however, also demands that we make some hard decisions. Continuing to support governments which routinely misuse money intended for the poor serves no one's interests in the long run. Neither does allocating aid resources in line with foreign policy goals that have nothing to do with poverty reduction. Justice also requires that aid workers are properly accountable for the money they spend and the decisions they make, something that in many organizations, both big and small, is far from the case.

Finally, we have to make some kind of assessment of the consequences of our actions. This is, to my mind, the hardest part of the question. As we've seen, opinions vary over the efficacy of aid *precisely because* it's hard to give a clear account of what kinds of actions will end up being the most helpful. For Sachs, the 'big push' approach holds the promise of radical growth for the poor. Easterly, by contrast, thinks that such a policy would disastrously repeat the mistakes of the past; instead, aid agencies should dismantle their monolithic utopian plans and concentrate on smaller, more carefully targeted actions. The reason that there's still such a live debate between such committed and intelligent people on the subject is that, in truth, nobody really *knows* what kinds of actions are reliably the most effective. There are theories, and there are strategies, but the task is so difficult and the data so hard to make sense of that there are likely to be disagreements about the right aid strategy for as long as there's poverty (and we have it on fairly good authority, of course, that the poor will always be with us).

This might seem like a terrible conclusion to end up with, and a block on there being any kind of meaningful progress on the issue. However, it's important not to mistake the lack of global consensus for the impossibility of being able to come to a firm conclusion yourself. Throughout this chapter I've tried to give a flavour of two different points of view. No doubt you've found one of them more persuasive, on balance, than the other. The important thing is that any position is properly informed by the facts, and is expressive of a good will.

There's one other consideration which might help focus our thoughts here. As part of the research for this book, I had a conversation with a senior official in a big aid agency working overseas. We discussed the various trials of working in the aid industry, and the general sense of pessimism that often sets in when any length of time has been spent grappling with the issues. For those who've spent a whole career trying to effect changes in places like Africa, it can seem dispiriting and disappointing when the scale of deprivation remains so stubbornly large.

He pointed out that it only makes sense to talk about success and failure when you have a clear idea of what you're aiming for. Many people, both inside and outside the aid industry, only have the vaguest sense of what they're actually trying to achieve, despite the plethora of published targets and objectives. If you believe the MDGs, of course, then everyone is trying to eradicate extreme poverty by 2015. However, even if those targets aren't hit, it's possible that aid has still performed many useful functions. How much worse might the situation be if aid workers *hadn't* been labouring for fifty-plus years to hold things together? If all that had been achieved was a rearguard action against utter collapse, might that not have been a valuable and important service? Perhaps, if we held the actions of the aid industry to less lofty goals, we might see more clearly the many successes they've accomplished, and give them more credit for the disasters averted.

This, it seems to me, is part of the great disservice that celebrity aid endorsers, such as Bob Geldof and Bono, perform (and, it must be said, Sachs himself). By giving credence to the notion that the donation of funds is sufficient by itself to transform very poor countries into flourishing economies in a short space of time, such tactics raise expectations of aid work to wholly unrealistic levels. If even just a few of Easterly's criticisms of the industry are close to the mark, then miraculous levels of growth aren't going to suddenly appear because of aid alone. It's no surprise that when the promises made by the celebrity cheerleaders for aid prove unobtainable, cynicism about *all* forms of aid subsequently sets in. So large-scale campaigns such as Live 8 and Make Poverty History, while they do an excellent job in raising awareness of development issues, exaggerate what aid can do and mask its shortcomings. Asked about Live 8, Richard Dowden, leader of the Royal African Society, summed up the problem: 'It's a good thing, in that the focus is on Africa. The danger is that it concentrates on one big push, and if you don't get what you are asking for, you are setting yourself up for disillusionment.'[30] As I mentioned at the start of this book, scepticism about aid is good; cynicism about it is not.

So where does that leave us? A very helpful – and very short – summary of these issues can be found in a paper by David Booth of the Overseas Development Institute.[31] His position, though not going into much detail, seems to me to strike the right balance. He starts by saying that,

All the evidence on past performance suggest that aid flows are not what makes the difference between successful developing countries and unsuccessful ones; aid can facilitate – it has never done more than that.

So far, so sceptical. He goes on, though:

> We don't just know that aid can be ineffective. We know quite a bit about why this is so – about the precise factors that limit the positive and accentuate the negative impacts of external assistance. [. . .] This is a real opportunity to make 2005 the year not just when aid volumes began to revive, but when the past relationship between aid quantity and aid quality was turned around.

The final point is the important one. Sachs, I think, is wrong to place so much faith in the sheer volume of aid. The more telling test is whether a given project avoids Easterly's set of drawbacks and is designed with the appropriate care and attention: sensitivity to the local environment, realistic goals, proper accountability channels, and so on. If it does, then it's surely worthy of our support.

We'll talk a bit more about the specifics of what we, as potential individual donors, might want to look for in a well-designed aid programme in the final chapter of this book. For now, we need to move on to the other important aspect of poverty reduction: the global system of trade. And here, thankfully, the ethical choices are much more clear-cut.

# 5 Trading

At the end of Chapter 1, we concluded our lightning survey of world economic history with the establishment of the Bretton Woods institutions and related bodies such as the WTO. As I noted then, the clear policy of the post-war rich world was to increase the volume of trade between its member countries and to end the spread of trading blocs and tariffs that had restricted trade flows. Over the subsequent half-century, progress towards those goals has been partial and fragmentary, but it's interesting to note how important trade has been in the pursuit of general economic growth. The belief expressed by the economists meeting in Bretton Woods was that the more trade there is, the more wealth there will be. For them, limiting trade, perhaps in the name of protecting certain important industries or groups, promised a return to poverty and depression. This is still, with some caveats and dissenters, the orthodoxy today.

The rich world's commitment to open trade has been controversial on its own account, even before we try to fit poor countries into the picture. The figures, however, are impressive. Under the post-war system, the volume of global trade in merchandise rose by 8 per cent every year between 1950 and 1973.[1] At the same time, the growth in world wealth also rose considerably. In East Asia in particular, the transformation from moribund agricultural economies to dynamic industrial powers was startling. The so-called Tiger Economies experienced rapid economic expansion in the

1980s and 1990s based on an aggressive export-led policy.[2] In Southeast Asia, over 20 per cent of the population lived on less than a dollar a day in the 1990s; in 2004, that figure was under 7 per cent.[3] In the immediate post-war period, Malaysia was on a par with many African countries in its economic output; in 1998, after decades of rapid growth, its exports nearly eclipsed those of the entire African continent.[4] Although there have been losers as well as winners, the growth in trade has, on balance, been very good for both the traditional rich world and the Asian newcomers.

It might seem obvious, then, that the best way for Africa to rid itself of poverty would be to tap into this burgeoning global trading system. Certainly, there's plenty more money to be taken advantage of. Global aid flows from rich countries amounted to around $84 billion in 2007;[5] in the same year, global merchandise exports alone were worth $13.6 trillion.[6] If the Tiger Economies could lift themselves out of poverty by creating vigorous export markets, shouldn't Africa do the same? Wouldn't such a policy make the debate over aid irrelevant?

We'll look at some of the opportunities and difficulties in generating growth through trade later in this chapter. However, it's striking that many organizations dedicated to working with the poor don't see trade as an opportunity, but as a threat. Meetings of the world's big trade bodies, notably the WTO and the G8, are routinely gate-crashed by protesters demanding a complete revision of the terms of worldwide trade. The process of ongoing liberalization is viewed not as a way of boosting growth for everyone, but as a cynical tool of the rich world to keep the poor in hoc to the products of multinational corporations. Feelings often run high, as they did most famously at the WTO's 1999 meeting in Seattle, Washington, where protesters and activists were involved in violent running clashes with the police, and negotiations over a fresh round of liberalization ended in failure.

Open, or free, trade is also viewed with scepticism by many aid agencies. I can remember, as a child, taking part in an exercise devised by a church-based charity in which several of us played a Monopoly-type game of trading. We were each given varying amounts of capital and instructed to try to grow our respective pools of cash as much as possible. The terms of the game were not fair at all: we were each given a share of resources proportionate to those of a selection of countries in the real world. The player with the resources of the United States had a lot of opportunities to make money, and those stuck with African countries had very few. The game wasn't much fun, because the poor countries couldn't win, no matter what they did: the system was stacked against them from the start. The United States, on the other hand, could do just about whatever it liked, and still make pots of money. The lesson was that the trading system was fundamentally unjust, and that radical reform was necessary to correct those imbalances. Aid, not free trade, was promoted as the way to help poor countries out of deprivation.

Who's right, the trade supporters or the trade-game devisers? As we'll see, both are. Trade can be a route out of poverty. In the long run, it's the only way to sustain a wealth-generating economy. The inchoate arguments of the activists who'd like to see a return to widespread economic protectionism are extremely damaging, as well as being entirely unrealistic (the world's not going backwards). But the current rules of the game are stacked heavily against the poorest countries in the world. Under the existing system, they're routinely lectured by the West about the need to open up their markets, even as the West retains punitive barriers around its own vulnerable industries. Poor countries are exposed to economic 'shock therapy' that wouldn't be tolerated in Europe or America, and given a poor hand to play at the world's top bargaining table, the WTO. Freer trade does hold the promise of liberating millions of people from poverty and transforming whole regions, but it will only come about if the rich world is serious about reforming itself too.

## FREEDOM AND PROTECTION

The basic ideas about trade and creating wealth have been around a long time. In general, trade is a voluntary arrangement – individuals or companies will only engage in it if they can see the prospect of making a profit. So when governments intervene to limit or prevent trade, they're theoretically preventing (potential) wealth creation, which is a bad thing. There may be justifications for intervention – the trading might have ruinous environmental costs, for instance, or generate unacceptable levels of inequality – but such limitations ought to perform a social good commensurate with the lost potential for wealth creation. Getting in the way of trade for no good reason is not something that governments ought to be doing.

Another well-established argument for governments keeping their nose out of trade is that of comparative advantage. Some groups of people in some parts of the world are better at making some kinds of things than others. It's usually cheaper, for example, to manufacture low-value items in China than it would be in central London. Ideally, efficient factories in China should concentrate on the things they're good at, whereas places like central London should concentrate on doing what they do best. Government interference, however, means that often countries end up producing things that they're not very good at. This may be for all sorts of reasons, such as national pride, or social cohesion, or because the work has important cultural resonance. To make the products from these industries saleable, the government may have to resort to protectionist measures, such as limiting imports from places where the work is done more efficiently or giving subsidies to domestic companies. For proponents of free trade, this ends up being bad for everyone. In the productive country, the potential for export sales of the product is lost and the opportunity for wealth creation is diminished. In the less productive country, resources are diverted away from potentially profitable pursuits to those that aren't.

This picture, suitably modified to take account of the complexities of the real world, is the one that most developed countries broadly subscribe to. There are of course differences of degree – as we'll see, many essentially capitalist economies still engage in substantial manipulation of trade for a variety of reasons – but there is a consensus that long-term prosperity relies on having reasonably unencumbered flows of trade and in specializing in what one's good at. These ideas have become so mainstream in the rich world that they have been given a name: the Washington Consensus, after the location of the IMF, the World Bank and the US Treasury. In its simplest form, this is the idea that the route to prosperity for any country lies in being open to trade, keeping laws regulating commerce to a minimum, and resisting government intervention in the markets.

In the 1990s, it was the Washington Consensus that was responsible for the imposition of instruments like structural adjustment loans. We've already seen that these loans sometimes had a terrible effect on African economies. One of the reasons for this was that the types of policies being advocated by the expatriate consultants were the purest, harshest and least nuanced forms of 'remedy'. In typical interventions, spending on things that the poor needed and wanted, such as health care and education, was slashed in order to bring down government spending to sustainable levels. At the same time, public ownership of companies was discouraged, and many concerns were placed in private hands. Tariffs on imports were cut, and subsidies withdrawn. The results in many cases were appalling, since the painful costs of restructuring were not compensated for, at least in the short term, by any noticeable economic benefit. Incomes continued to fall, and only a select few benefited from the resultant opportunities for enrichment. This wasn't just the case in Africa: the sudden switch in Russia from communism to capitalism in the 1990s caused enormous upheaval, sent living standards plummeting for millions, and made a select coterie of officials very rich indeed. The effects in Africa, however, were particularly destructive.

You might conclude from this that the free trade argument is fatally flawed, and that the only way to keep poverty for the masses at bay is to substantially limit and regulate access to the global market. However, before we leap to that conclusion, it's important to see *why* freeing up trade was so attractive to the economists of the Washington Consensus. It was not, despite what the shrillest critics of the anti-capitalist activist movement say, that they wanted to keep Africa poor and maximize the profits of Shell, Halliburton and IBM. On the contrary, they had seen what worked in their own countries and tried to use the same recipe in Africa. And, just as the old imperialists had found, trying to shoehorn too much, too quickly into a profoundly different cultural environment led to unfortunate consequences. However, the basic principles of less restrictive, more open trade still hold considerable promise, as long as the playing field is suitably level.

The first argument in favour of greater trade liberalization returns to a point we made earlier, that government bureau- crats are often pretty bad at running successful companies. This is true in the poor world just as much as it is in the rich. In the years following independence, many African countries adopted highly interventionist economic models, with heavy govern- ment involvement in major industries, which were then run extremely poorly. Despite the fact that core income-generating companies were being hammered into the ground, officials were indifferent or hostile to other ventures, especially in agri- culture (an area, in theory, where Africa ought to have some- thing of a competitive advantage). Because of this influence, foreign investors (as opposed to aid agencies) generally looked elsewhere. Whereas East Asia was very successful in attracting foreign capital, investors in Africa often limped away from their ventures, frustrated at continual interference, incompetence or obstruction.

Anyone with experience of working in Africa, African or other- wise, will tell you that one of the key impediments to running a business is the high level of government interference. Although, during the 1980s, global levels of foreign investment outpaced the growth in world trade by a significant margin, investors went almost anywhere but Africa, frightened off by 'dizzying taxes, outlandish regulations, administrative inertia, the legal system, the labour code [. . .], monopolies, corruption, and fraud.'[7]

Of these, corruption and fraud are worthy of special mention. Alongside simple incompetence, government involvement in trade flows presents powerful opportunities for corruption. This is particularly the case with tariff barriers. In many cases, countries choose to limit imports or exports by imposing fees on crossborder movements. These monies need to be collected and registered by officials at ports and border crossings. Even in developed countries with advanced communications and well-resourced law enforcement agencies, monitoring the process is difficult. One of the reasons international tariffs have been lowered so much in recent years has been the desire to remove the corruption and waste associated with their processing.

In Africa the problem remains acute. Customs officials have a powerful temptation to augment their official incomes by adding extra 'conditions' on the transit of goods. Bribes may be demanded, and failure to pay may incur delays or confiscation. Certain companies might be favoured, while others find themselves shut out of markets entirely. For the border officials, the rewards for being in a position of such power are potentially massive. In Madagascar, the bribe to get a place at the institution that trains customs officers is fifty times the country's annual income per head. As Paul Collier remarks, 'that tells you all you need to know about the customs service in Madagascar.'[8]

This level of obstruction, whether through corruption or simple bureaucratic inefficiency, matters. It prevents goods moving about at a reasonable speed, and discourages investment by both locals and outsiders. It drives up the cost of doing business, and hence the cost of essential products. Customs clearance in many European countries typically takes a day or two, whereas the average customs transaction in a poor African country can involve up to 30 days, 30 people, 40 separate documents, 200 data elements, where 30 of which have to be repeated at least 30 times.[9] High trade barriers also make countries reliant on the income from tariffs, making it harder to alter the fiscal balance as global economic circumstances change – African governments' revenue from tariffs is, on average, over 5 per cent of GDP, compared to around 0.3 per cent in developed countries.[10]

In addition, trade barriers combined with high inflows of aid can cause structural problems for a poor country's economy. Aid is generally delivered in dollars or euros. As the supply of this foreign currency within the local market increases, demand for it will fall and the local currency will appreciate against it. This benefits consumers of imported goods (often those at the top of economic pyramid), but makes life difficult for exporters, whose income in dollars or euros is now worth less. This situation is made more acute as long as there are effective barriers to trade, since it will be hard to stimulate any domestic demand for imports. If barriers to trade are lowered, the cost of imports will fall, triggering extra domestic demand. If the level of demand for imports keeps pace with the injection of foreign exchange provided by aid, then the economy will be able to manage the inflows without recourse to exchange-rate appreciation. If trade barriers remain high, then large inflows of aid can cripple exporters' competitiveness, and hence ruin their chances of trading their way out of poverty.[11]

This is important, because the economic growth in East Asia was triggered by an export boom. By being open to foreign direct investment, countries that had African levels of poverty in the mid twentieth century managed to modernize their economies and substantially reduce extreme deprivation by the turn of the millennium. Although, as we concluded in the previous chapter, there's no prospect of aid being withdrawn from Africa, it's clear that the long-term solution for the continent involves becoming more integrated into the global system of trade, not more isolated from it. The consequences of staying outside have been pretty severe, as Robert Calderisi, in *The Trouble with Africa*, writes,

> Africa has not been a victim of globalization. With only a few excep-
> tions, it has refused to concern itself with foreign markets. This may
> reassure those who believe that trade is undesirable, but also confirms
> that most of Africa's handicaps are inbred. The continent has both wit-
> tingly and unwittingly walled itself off from the rest of the world, with
> the result that its economy is now rather small – barely the size of
> Argentina's. [. . .] By 2000, the typical African economy had an income
> no larger than the suburb of a major American city. [. . .] The World
> Bank's headquarters uses more electricity to light its offices than is
> consumed in the whole of Chad, a country twice the size of France.[12]

## A STACKED DECK

If this is true, though, why are so many activists so adamantly
opposed to greater trade liberalization? Are they simply ignorant
of the issues, or blinded by anti-capitalist dogma? They're not, at
least not all the time. As noted above, free trade can only work
when the playing field is level. If tariff barriers come down in
Africa, then they have to come down everywhere. If rich countries
are free to export goods to poor countries, then it has to work the
other way too: the poor countries must be able to export goods to
the rich ones. And it's here where the rhetoric on free trade really
comes apart from the reality. Rich countries have repeatedly
rigged the rules to protect their own industries while preaching
the benefits of open markets. There are many examples of outrageous hypocrisy in international relations, but the double standard over trade is perhaps the worst.

Recall what we said at the start of this chapter. One of the key
principles of free trade is comparative advantage: countries ought
to stick to making what they're good at, and import what they're
not. Despite its many problems, there are a few things that Africa
could be good at making. Unlike the developed world, agriculture
still makes up a large part of Africa's economic activity. Although

there are significant impediments to making this pay (such as poor transport links to the rest of the world), in principle agricultural produce ought to be something Africa could sell to the rest of the world. The continent has very low labour costs, lots of space, and (in places) fertile soil and an ideal climate. By contrast, developed countries like the US, Japan and those of the EU are highly urbanized and have very high labour costs. What's stopping Africans from making the best use of their comparative advantage in agriculture?

One of the answers is that rich-country markets are heavily protected. European and American city dwellers like having a picturesque countryside to visit. They like the rolling fields and the neat, small-scale farms on them. Despite the fact that the goods these farms produce could often be made more cheaply in Africa even after factoring in transport costs, rich-country citizens don't want to put their own farmers out of business. As a result, rich countries create heavy tariff barriers on the import of agricultural products, and pay their farmers large subsidies for production. The figures involved boggle the mind. The whole of Africa gets around $25 billion every year in development assistance. Of this, about $22 billion comes from the so-called Organisation for Economic Co-operation and Development (OECD) club of countries, which includes all the major industrial powers. According to the OECD's own figures, in 2003, these same countries spent $350 billion supporting their domestic agriculture in the form of subsidies, maintaining market barriers, various training activities for farmers and officials, promotion and marketing. That's *sixteen* times the aid budget to Africa.[13] In the face of such huge disparities in spending, it's perhaps no wonder that African trade has failed to make much of an impact on the world marketplace.

The presence of such large barriers to the flow of trade is a good example of how government interventions can have perverse consequences. For political reasons, taxpayer money in rich-world countries is used to prop up expensive parts of the economy that, in themselves, constitute a tiny proportion of all productive activity. This is pretty bad for rich-world consumers, as it pushes up the prices of goods. It's ruinously bad for the poor countries, though, as it stymies any chance they might have had at competing in the market sectors they have some chance of doing well in.

Of course, there are some complicating factors. Many OECD countries have negotiated a series of treaties with poor countries on a piecemeal basis, exempting them from the worst barriers to entry. Some of these agreements have been based on historical ties, such as those provided by colonialism. These are called 'preference schemes', and they often allow the poorest countries to export their produce to protected markets tariff-free. This still pits them against rich-country domestic producers with access to big subsidies and marketing budgets, but at least removes some of the most obvious obstacles to entry. For example, the EU's 'Everything But Arms' scheme allows imports of most commodities (except armaments) to the EU tariff-free, and the African Growth and Opportunity Act (AGOA) scheme allows some products to enter the US market with improved access.[14] Although a somewhat inelegant solution, both preference schemes are intended to militate against the worst effects of rich-world tariff barriers.

In practice, though, they only improve things somewhat. There are three reasons for this. First, tariff schemes are often weighted against the import of processed goods, rather than raw commodities. For example, the tariff barriers on importation of unroasted coffee beans to Japan is zero. But Japan's tariff barrier for coffee preparations (the finished product) is up to 112 per cent.[15] This matters, because most of the economic value is generated, not by the raw commodity, but by the final stages of production. Exporting unprocessed coffee beans does generate some revenue, but it would be far better to process the beans locally and export the finished product – the return would be far greater. Some preference schemes, particularly those in the EU, address this problem by retaining low or zero tariffs for finished goods. However, this was not always the case in the past, and there are still punitive 'escalation' tariffs in place in other developed countries.

Second, preference schemes are extremely bureaucratic and difficult to negotiate. Among the main reasons for this are the 'rules of origin' – a set of conditions for establishing where a product actually originates. In theory, these rules make a lot of sense. In the global marketplace, goods may be assembled in a whole range of countries before heading off to their final destination. If a poor country, say Uganda, is to benefit from a preference scheme, it's important to ensure that the goods it exports actually originate from Uganda, and were not just finished off there after the bulk of the work was done in, say, China. In practice, however, the rules of origin are extremely difficult to comply with. Rich countries can impose whatever conditions they like, and have no incentive to make it easy for poor countries to meet them. As a result, the costs of compliance can be just as onerous as a high tariff barrier would be. The exporter may have to overhaul its accounting system in order to meet the requirements of the scheme, or may be unable to take advantage of sufficiently low-cost raw material imports to make their goods competitive.[16] Poor countries often suspect that preference scheme rules have been designed explicitly to prevent their exports being viable; though it *looks* like there are no artificial barriers to entry, in practice, the deck is still stacked against them.

The final problem with preference schemes is that most economists expect them to provide only temporary respites. Though there are real benefits to African countries in having preferential access to some big markets, the general trend in worldwide trade is for universal tariff reduction. Though it may not happen soon, it's likely that barriers to movement of goods will gradually come down across the board. For the reasons we discussed earlier, this has the potential to be a very good thing for everyone – it will mean less market distortion, and allow the rich world fewer opportunities to shut out goods for political reasons. In the long term, it's a move that Africa can benefit from. In the short term, however, it would be a disaster. This is because Africa's infrastructure is so weak and its capacity for growth so fragile that it would quickly be out-competed by virtually every other trading country. The challenge from Asia, in particular, where labour costs are still relatively low, would be very hard to meet. Preference schemes certainly don't solve all of Africa's trading woes, but their sudden removal would make things even more difficult.

## MAKING GLOBALIZATION WORK FOR THE POOR

At this point, it may seem that African countries are pretty heavily penalized whatever happens. They don't derive any benefits from being shut off from the world economy; they're hobbled by trade barriers and complex rules of origin; and they're poorly positioned for a further round of liberalization. Trade, far from being a possible solution to the problem of poverty, looks rather like just one more way for the rest of the world to outpace Africa.

The problem, as we noted above, is that the system of open trading isn't going away – the benefits are too great for too many. Simply refusing to play the game, as some of the more radical 'fair trade' activists endorse, is no solution. Africa needs commerce with the rest of the world in order to thrive, and shutting down opportunities for trade would lead to an even deeper erosion of wealth. This has been recognized by the mainstream development establishment for some time. In one of the best and most influential documents on aid policy in recent years – the 2000 White Paper on International Development entitled 'Making Globalisation Work for the Poor' – the British government sets out its general approach:

> The UK Government believes that, if well managed, the benefits of globalisation for poor countries and people can substantially outweigh the costs, especially in the longer term. The rapid integration of the global economy, combined with advances in technology and science, is creating unprecedented global prosperity. And this has helped lift millions of people out of poverty. With the right policies, many millions more people can benefit in the years ahead.[17]

The White Paper publishes research suggesting that open economies do far better over the long term than non-open economies.
Eighteen countries that opened their borders to trade in the
period between the 1960s and the 1990s (including poor countries like Uganda, Bangladesh and Ghana) saw their growth rates
rise from about 1 per cent to over 5 per cent. Other developing
countries that chose to retain high trade barriers went from rates
of around 2 per cent in the 1960s to zero.[18] Despite this, there are
significant risks that, as with the imposition of structural adjustment loans, most of the poor will miss out on the benefits of
growth. The difficult task facing the world is to help African countries take advantage of opportunities for increased trade in such a
way that the poorest continue to have access to the essential
services they need. The challenge, as reflected in the White Paper's
title, is to make globalization work for the poor.

There are at least three ways in which this might be achieved.
All are difficult, all require substantial concessions to be made by
the rich world, and all require significant reform in the poor world.
However, only by making thorough-going and painful changes
will developing countries be able to trade their way out of
poverty.

First, the industrialized countries must take their moral responsibilities far more seriously. That means dismantling tariffs that
unfairly penalize poor countries, ending complicated rules that
have the same effect, and bringing an end to bullying tactics
that deprive African countries of the resources to compete. I have
had the misfortune to see for myself how the big trading blocs
can abuse their position to destroy the competitiveness of African
countries. The worst example, in my experience, is the negotiation
of fishing rights in African waters.

Just as with agriculture, the EU subsidizes its fishery sector
heavily. The Common Fisheries Policy, one of the most massively
perverse policies in the world, has been responsible for the
destruction of fish stocks in European waters and for a hugely
expensive subsidy of a tiny part of the EU's economy. This terrible

system has had the effect of making imports of fish from better-run parts of the world more expensive, and also makes it harder for African fishermen to compete on anything like an equal footing. Most destructively of all, the EU spends millions of taxpayers' euros on fishing deals with African countries. Having stripped their own waters of stocks, Europeans now pay to fish in the relatively bountiful seas off African countries.

The methods by which these agreements are negotiated are only slightly short of criminal. European boats pay little to local governments and catch far more than their quotas allow. In any case, the quotas are generally set far above replacement levels, meaning that sustainable tracts of ocean soon resemble the barren wastes of European waters. The inability of African governments to negotiate effectively with such powerful interests, coupled on occasions by the connivance of corrupt officials, means that the local population ends up with a terrible deal. Faced with industrial fishing boats capable of sucking up vast quantities of fish, the indigenous, small-scale operations are driven out of business. Aside from the loss of potential export markets, the destruction of the African fish industry has terrible effects for the local poor, for whom fish is an important staple. It also has serious side effects for world commerce: the growth in piracy off the African coasts is partly due to the local fisherman having been hustled away from a legitimate trade.

As I noted earlier, the sums of money involved in rich-world trade barriers are huge, often dwarfing aid budgets. The EU spends almost $300 million a year supporting these destructive fishing fleets (and much more subsidizing fishing operations in its own waters). If that money were simply withdrawn and handed back to the EU taxpayer, everyone would benefit: EU citizens would be free of a pointless burden, and the Africans would have a chance to fish their own waters free of interference. Rather than lobbying for a reimposition of trade barriers, charities would do better to argue for the removal of protectionist policies that disadvantage the poor and divert funds into non-productive activities. This would certainly cause short-term pain for rich-world economies: farmers and fishermen would lose their jobs. However, they would also have the opportunities to find alternative work in some of the richest and most abundant economies in the world; African farmers and fishermen have no such alternative employment.

Is this likely to happen in the short term? No, as the WTO, at least until very recently, has been an organization designed around rich-country priorities. Its origins, as we've seen, lie in the post-war reconstruction of advanced economies. From 1947 until the 1970s, the emphasis was firmly on trade between industrialized powers, and the focus was almost purely on tariff barriers in finished goods. Only in the 1980s, as WTO membership swelled from the original twenty-three countries to over a hundred, did the concerns of developing countries get a look in. Even after poor countries were allowed a place at the table, though, their interests were not well served by the steady stream of treaties and agreements. Though tariff reductions during the 1990s were made with the intention (in part) of benefiting poor countries, in practice, the developed world did far better from the deals struck. Some studies indicate that sub-Saharan Africa may have lost up to $1.2 billion as a result of decisions made during the 1993 round of discussions in Uruguay.[19]

The key to improving results for the poor countries at the WTO is to improve their negotiating position. Advanced economies are able to devote massive amounts of expertise and resources towards their delegations. Trade is big business, and so it's worth spending a lot of time and effort to protect the gains made at meetings. By contrast, African countries often have very poor representation. Levels of training in economics are relatively low in many African countries, and negotiators may be hobbled by the policies of their resource-starved (or sometimes corrupt) political masters. In recent years this has improved, as developing countries have banded together to form blocs within the WTO dedicated to pushing for a fairer deal. The arrangements are far from perfect, since the interests of, say, China and India have little in common with those of Chad or Burundi. However, the process can be built on. Aid agencies, as some already do, could spend time advising poor countries on how to maximize their bargaining positions. At present, many African countries strike an unhappy balance between rejecting all new trade deals (stung, no doubt, by their treatment in the past) and arguing for unrealistic and sweeping reforms that no rich country could ever agree to. Aid agencies could improve this situation by making the case for enhanced trade terms that benefit the poor, and assisting developing countries with the expertise to argue their corner.

This process will not be easy. Trade negotiations, unlike spending decisions in the aid industry, are essentially concerned with barter – countries are only interested in conceding something in exchange for something else. Poor countries usually have very little to offer, and so it can seem as if any overtures on their part are doomed to failure. However, it would be better for everyone in the world if extreme poverty were wiped out, both in a moral sense and in a commercial one. It would benefit rich countries to have richer and deeper trading ties with poor ones – by opening up their markets to imports, they would also be fostering new markets for their exports. That's why it makes sense to have a 'development round' of trade talks, with the emphasis firmly on ways to correct the obscene imbalances in world flows of commerce.

It also makes sense for African countries to engage properly with the WTO, rather than hoping that going it alone will somehow improve the situation. In theory, having a single international policeman for world trade strengthens protection for weaker members of the international community. If the WTO were working properly, it would prevent the worst bullying abuses, such as that of the EU's external fishing fleet, and ensure that the rules were evenly applied. It would also remove the need for African countries to belong to such a dizzying array of local trading blocs (such as CEMAC, COMESA, ECCAS, ECOWAS, SADC, WAEMU, EAC,

IGAD, SACU . . . the list goes on) and concentrate on building up their global presence.

The final problem to address is that of capacity. Even if import tariffs were dismantled overnight and favourable rules drawn up at a global level, many African countries would still not be able to take advantage of the market opportunities. Both their infrastructures and their skills bases are too low to scale up exports rapidly. In the short term, they would be out-competed by more developed, low labour-cost economies like those of Asia. This is where more traditional forms of aid can help. Rich countries, working in genuine partnership with poor ones, have the resources to fund infrastructure improvements and to train business leaders. As long as the delivery of such aid is sensitive to local needs and conditions (bearing in mind Easterly's criticisms about utopian planning and neo-imperialism) and is conducted in genuine partnership with African business leaders and communities, then it has a chance of success.

In addition, there is a case for extending and simplifying the current preference schemes for trade. If the restrictive rules of origin were replaced with simpler and more generous terms, then there is a role for them to play. Africa would not be well served by a sudden 'shock therapy' shift into the global free market – it needs to benefit from continued preferential terms and a degree of protection from the full force of competition until its markets have grown strong enough to weather the storm.

If measures like these were adopted at subsequent WTO meetings, then Africa would have a fighting chance of generating its own wealth, rather than needing to rely on the charity of others. The economists Joseph Stiglitz and Andrew Charlton, writing in their book *Fair Trade for All*, argue for the following reforms:

1. All WTO members commit themselves to providing free market access in all goods to all developing countries poorer and smaller than themselves. Thus all developing countries could

        expect free access to all markets with (a) a larger GDP and (b) a
        larger GDP per head;

2. Developed countries commit themselves to the elimination of agri-
    cultural subsidies; and

3. The promise of market opening not be undermined by technical
    provisions like rules of origin.[20]

Only with these kinds of radical changes will poor countries be
able to compete on something like a level playing field with rich
ones.

## FAIR TRADE AND MICROCREDIT

So far, most of our discussion has centred on the 'macro' side of
trade – the global flow of goods and services, and the regulatory
framework in which it operates. This may strike you as rather
remote from the level of individual action, both in the rich and
poor worlds. Although it's all very well to discuss the impact of
trade on an international level, what about measures that work at
the smaller scale?

One increasingly well-known strategy for improving the prospects of agricultural producers in the developing world is the 'fair
trade' scheme. This involves paying producers above-market rates
for their produce so that they can earn a living wage. The fair trade
movement arose out of concerns that large buyers of staples such
as coffee, cocoa and sugar were able to purchase raw materials at
very low prices due to their power in the marketplace. This led to
the farming of such commodities becoming increasingly uneconomic, and hence having little positive impact on the local economy. The fair trade campaign was started to encourage responsible
purchasers to pay more than they needed to (in strict market
terms) in order to improve returns for the developing country's
farmers. The premium would be covered by higher prices for the
end consumer, who would be willing to pay extra as a form of

charitable donation. The scheme has grown from relatively small origins to the extent where it's a familiar part of the consumer economy in many rich countries. Large companies, such as Cadburys in the UK, are proud to label their products 'fair trade' and make much of the scheme's contribution to poverty alleviation.

The fair trade programme acts somewhat like a preference scheme, in that products from developing countries get special treatment. However, its impact is rather less noticeable. Even with its widespread adoption in countries like the UK, fair trade products account for a very small proportion of all goods sold. They also have the unfortunate side effect of discouraging producers from diversifying into products with a more sustainable economic future. As we've seen, African countries have been exporting commodities like coffee for a very long time. One of the reasons that's not brought prosperity is the huge price differential between the raw materials and the finished product. It's possible that, by encouraging farmers to continue growing coffee beans and selling them to international purchasers, the fair trade scheme actually prevents diversification into more profitable activities. It's also possible that fair trade prevents the largely small-scale farmers from becoming more efficient (by banding together into larger units, say), since they can receive above-market rates for produce grown in a rather inefficient way.

For these reasons, fair trade is only ever going to be a partial, temporary palliative for Africa's trading weakness. It doesn't hold the prospect of transforming the terms of trade between rich and poor, whatever its more ardent advocates might say. However, with that caveat in mind, it seems to me that the project isn't actively harmful. In a localized fashion, such schemes no doubt do significant good, allowing small-scale producers to enjoy a decent return from their labour, and avoiding the worst ravages of unfettered corporate practice. If it's seen for what it is – a moderate dose of charitable giving on top of the price of a bag of coffee – then it's certainly a relatively easy way of alleviating some aspects of poverty in producer countries.

Another small-scale project that's generated a lot of attention is microcredit. The most famous example of this is the Grameen Bank in Bangladesh, started by the entrepreneur Mohammed Yunus. As with the fair trade movement, microcredit schemes arose from the observation that poor people had serious trouble getting loans to start up businesses. If they did succeed in finding a sources of money, the interest rates were often punitively high. As a result, profits were tiny and exploitation rife. Just as loan sharks are able to prey on the most vulnerable members of developed societies, exploitative moneylenders had free rein to charge whatever they liked, often backed up with threats and extortion.

In rich countries, small businesses aren't forced to go to loan sharks and can borrow money at sustainable rates from regulated banks. For a long time, however, banks in developing countries ignored the demand for credit from the poorest. It was assumed that their skills were too low to make a success of any enterprise, that the money would be wasted, or that they would default readily when the going got tough. After studying how poor people actually made use of credit, Yunus's observation was that rates of default were usually very low, and that many were perfectly capable of using the assistance to maintain viable business models. Freed from the need to borrow money at ruinous rates and with poor levels of predictability, small-scale businesses could plan for the future and invest in equipment. Moreover, peer pressure from other borrowers meant that rates of default were very low. Although the sums of money were very small – much too small for regular banks to concern themselves with – they made a real difference to the recipients, enabling them to enter a virtuous circle of wealth creation. Microcredit lenders acted, in a very small way, rather like the large-scale aid agencies of Sachs' vision – effecting the step change necessary to break the vicious circle of capital scarcity. Unlike the grand vision of aid advocated by Sachs, however, such projects operate on a very small scale, with modest goals, and demonstrably favourable results.

Like fair trade, microcredit by itself won't transform poor economies. The sums of money are too small, and the infrastructure and skills problems will still remain. However, initiatives like it make an appreciable difference to the plight of the poor. They enable those with sufficient talent and determination to climb out of the poverty trap and begin to generate wealth for themselves and their communities. While the overall set of conditions for trade remains so challenging in Africa, it's initiatives like this that offer the best chance of improving trading conditions for those at the bottom. The only long-term solution, though, is to change the worldwide rules to give them a fair chance of realizing their full potential. And that, sadly, is a task for governments.

That doesn't mean, of course, that you, as an individual, have no chance of making a difference. Most of the rich world is democratic, with real (albeit imperfect) channels of communication between politicians and ordinary citizens. There are ways of contributing to the fight against poverty at an individual level – perhaps by supporting a small charity, or by buying fair trade products – and also at a collective level – by lobbying governments to change their policies on trade and aid, or by supporting a big charity with political objectives close to yours. It may be that after reading all of the above, you have very clear ideas of what, practically, it would be best to do. Perhaps you already had clear ideas, and this book has done nothing to change them. It may be, however, that our discussion of ethics, aid and trade still leaves you without a clear sense of what the right kinds of responses are. In the next chapter, then, I'll attempt to pull together the threads and suggest some ways in which the theoretical considerations we've looked at might inform our decisions in the real world.

# 6   A More Equal World

So much for all the difficulties and conundrums surrounding aid and trade. It's time to bring the threads together, and offer some thoughts on how things might possibly get better.

The first point to make is that there are very good reasons to believe that things can get better. Cynicism about development issues, as I mentioned earlier, is neither helpful nor warranted. Enormous strides have been made over the past fifty years in lifting millions of people out of poverty. The difficult job is to decide how much of that uplift has been as a result of improved policies by local governments, international aid efforts, reforms in the trade system, or a combination of all of those things. The job of assigning credit is also complicated by cultural factors – what worked in South Korea, for example, may never work in, say, Uganda because of irreducible differences in the way those societies are constructed. However, there are things that can be done, and good reasons to suppose that a more equal world is a reasonable prospect for the future.

It's important first to note the changing geopolitical situation. As we've seen, the era of colonialism, and the Cold War that followed it, were ruinous for poor countries. Third World countries were prevented from making any of their own decisions, and those made for them by outsiders were – at best – variable in their effects. Though power across the globe remains clustered in a few centres, the period of explicit colonization is over, and developing countries are more influential within international bodies than they've ever been. While rising powers such as India and China may well end up making the same mistakes as the old powers of Europe and the United States, at least the number of voices in international forums is growing. In the long term, it's surely a good thing that the billions of people living in the global south have adequate and effective representation. Aid and development issues are constant features of global economic discussions in a way that they weren't during much of the twentieth century, which offers some hope that better answers will be found in the future than have been found in the past.

There are challenges, of course. The recent economic downturn is likely to depress efforts of rich countries to maintain greater aid spending, and the prospect of a new cold war between the democratic West and a radicalized Islamic world should make any sensible person shudder. Progress against poverty can be reversed far more quickly than it can be achieved, and the ease with which gains can be eroded in places like Africa is frightening. If the Millennium Development Goals are to be met, or even approached, then there needs to be major reform to the way aid is delivered and trade is governed.

The first necessary change has to do with 'expectation management'. Despite what Bono and Bob Geldof might indicate in the heat of the moment, grants of cash from rich-world inhabitants to those in the global south are never going to eradicate poverty on their own. The sums are too small to make a difference in the long term, and there are too many complicating factors – such as corrupt recipient governments and poor infrastructure – for the money to do the work they promise it can. It serves no one's interests to pretend that poverty can be 'made history' by energetic campaigns lasting a year or two. A lot of wristbands will be sold in such efforts, and some good may be done, but people will rightly feel cheated when the true challenges of development become apparent once the party's over.

That's not to say that the people who support such efforts are foolish or completely deluded. When the now-famous pictures of famine in Ethiopia were flashed across television screens through-out the industrialized world in the 1980s, it was understandable that outrage motivated so many to contribute to the subsequent campaigns. Similar exercises, such as the campaign to provide relief for the victims of the Indian Ocean tsunami or the earth-quake in Haiti, were also laudable. Humanitarian missions in the face of such overwhelming suffering are the compassionate, decent response, one any moral person should support. However, it's misleading to suggest that such actions are, by themselves, capable of lifting regions out of poverty in the long term. They are worthwhile actions in response to natural disaster, but they're no substitute for the long-haul of lasting development.

If simple money transfer isn't the answer, though, what is? Dif-ferent kinds of aid delivery certainly are part of the solution. Here again, expectation management is in order. I'm not aware of any country that has become prosperous solely because of aid, even if assistance has been delivered over the very long term and expertly managed. We do, however, need to bear in mind what the world might look like without the efforts of the established aid agencies. In the country I'm most familiar with, Malawi, the current level of suffering would have been many times more acute if the patient, arduous efforts of aid professionals over half a century had never been made. When you've witnessed, as I have, a potentially devas-tating famine averted due to the actions of a few extremely dedi-cated officials working around the clock to secure grain supplies, it's difficult not to feel that such efforts deserve more praise than they receive in a cynical rich-world media.

If we have realistic goals for aid, and see the delivery of grants, loans and expertise as a part of a wider picture, then we'll be in a better position to assess any given policy's strengths and weak-nesses. An absence of cynicism should not blind us to the real flaws in the current system, though: some of Easterly's criticisms are pertinent. Aid agencies don't always help themselves, and some are deserving of Paul Theroux's withering judgement of them. There have been too many occasions when aid workers have been overbearing and arrogant, and quick to impose extremely ambitious schemes on countries with very weak governments, knowing full well that they'll share no accountability for any subsequent failures. If you read any of the many academic papers on aid effectiveness, you'll see endless pleas for more humility and for a greater partnership between expatriate bureaucrats and their hosts. Sometimes these pleas are heeded; sometimes they're not.

One of the reasons that aid agencies so often ride roughshod over the wishes of the local government, of course, is that domestic officials can be corrupt or chronically incompetent. So there's a responsibility, too, on the side of the recipients of aid. Many countries in Africa are now democracies, however imperfectly implemented, and so there's a functioning link between the people and those who represent them (as there wasn't, for example, during the colonial period). African countries will never become prosperous unless despots and criminals are removed from office, and that will take a change of cultural attitudes by those that elect or support them. Structural aid should never be maintained for leaders in the mould of Mobutu Sese Seko, as it has been in the past. However, where there are glimmers of hope for change, as there are across much of Africa, the relatively new approach adopted by aid agencies of working with governments should be encouraged. It's difficult work, with plenty of risk attached, but ultimately it offers more hope than working around local administrations.

As indicated in Chapter 5, the biggest single reform that rich countries can make is to the system of international trade. Because the volume of trade is so much greater than that of aid, there's little point in sending money to poor countries if they're prevented from making money on their own – such a policy does little more than paper over the structural cracks between the strongest and weakest. New 'trade rounds' need to establish fairer rules for international commerce. That means ending punitive tariffs and the excessively complicated rules of origin on imports into rich-world markets. At the same time, aid money should be spent on helping African governments gear up their economies for export so that they can take advantage of the new opportunities. A significant part of aid budgets should be used for infrastructure to reduce the costs involved in transporting goods from the African interior to the coast and representation at international bodies like the WTO and IMF should reflect the interests of all members, not just those with the longest historical involvement.

Even if such measures are enacted, the task remains daunting. The growth rates required for African countries to catch the rest of the world up are extremely high, and they would have to be sustained for a generation or more before the wealth gap would begin to shrink. Maintaining economic vitality and a reasonable degree of equality is something that even developed economies struggle with, and they have the advantage of extremely well-resourced bureaucracies staffed by extremely well-educated officials. There will probably be parts of the world that are never able to shrug off endemic poverty, whether as a result of their isolated position, lack of any natural resources, or some other factor. For those places, humanitarian aid will be required for the long-haul, just as it is today across vast areas of Africa and Central Asia. Most of the world can do better, however, and improvements in aid delivery, combined with a fairer system of international commerce, hold the promise of shrinking the 'bottom billion' – those people locked in absolute poverty – even further.

## WHAT CAN YOU DO?

Such measures need to take place on a global scale. It may seem as if you don't have much to do with that at all. The deliberations of officials at the IMF or DFID have enormous impacts on the economies of Africa, but they can seem distant and hard to influence.

This impression is only partially correct. The explosion of interest in development issues was stimulated in large part by public pressure. Thousands of small charities made representations to their governments over the level of aid they were providing to the poor world. Politicians, with an eye on their prospects for re-election, had to take account of that growing group of interested people. A more interconnected world means that more ordinary people have access to more information than ever before. They're also able to communicate their opinions quickly and easily, leaving their elected representatives in no doubt of what the important issues are. Getting involved is less difficult now than it's been at any time in history, and the chance of contributing to a movement that has real impact is there for the taking.

Throughout this book, I've tried not to recommend one specific set of policies over another, but rather to introduce a range of arguments and positions that have been influential in current debates. It's up to you to decide which approaches you think are the most likely to do good in the world and are worthy of your support. With that in mind, I'll conclude this section with a collection of very broad points:

- Any advocate of aid who promises to make poverty 'history' in a very short space of time should be viewed with extreme caution. The issues are complex, and there's no agreement, even among experts, on what the best way of helping the poorest in the world is.
- That doesn't mean that efforts by the rich world to help the poor world should be abandoned. On the contrary, it means that we should continue to work towards better ways of managing the global economy, paying attention to all the many difficulties as we do so.
- Information is essential. As potential donors, one of the responsibilities we have is to be properly informed about what we're doing. If we donate money to a cause without knowing a lot about how it will be spent, who will spend it, or how it will be

accounted for, we run the risk that it will be wasted. As we've seen, not all donations have good effects: we need to think intelligently about which causes we want to support.

- Individuals have a role in shaping policy. Though issues such as the world trade system can seem abstract and remote, they are vitally important. If you don't know what the policy of your elected representative is on this, you could find out. Once you know what it is, you can make choices about whether to support that representative or whether to campaign for an alternative.

- Individuals can also get directly involved with smaller charities, particularly if they have specific talents or expertise that may be lacking in places like Africa. As with larger organizations, information is of paramount importance. Some charities work hard to be sensitive to the local culture and environment, account for their spending, coordinate with the local authorities, and think about the effects of their actions. Some don't. A little research can reveal a lot about any given charity, so it's imperative to do some work before reaching for your cash.

International development is one of the most pressing issues of our time, and is likely to remain so for a generation or more. Whatever your views on what's best to do, it's not something that can be ignored. I hope this introduction to the subject has given a flavour of the important considerations, and also put them in a philosophical and a practical context. In case it's provided you with an impetus to find out more, see the next section for my recommendations for further reading.

## AID AND DEVELOPMENT

There are many books on aid and development, most of which argue strongly for more of it or strongly for less of it. The most important proponent of more aid is Jeffrey Sachs in *The End of Poverty: How We Can Make It Happen in Our Lifetime* (London: Penguin, 2005). Another important academic study of the importance of aid is Amartya Sen's *Development as Freedom* (Oxford: Oxford University Press, 2001).

One of the more balanced and thoughtful accounts is Paul Collier's *The Bottom Billion* (Oxford: Oxford University Press, 2007), whose conclusions are somewhat similar to mine. Much of the rest of the literature on aid is quite critical. William Easterly's *The White Man's Burden: Why the West's Efforts to Aid the Rest Have Done So Much Ill and So Little Good* (Oxford: Oxford University Press, 2006) is controversial but important, and very engagingly written. Robert Calderisi's *The Trouble with Africa* (New Haven: Yale University Press, 2007) is also worth reading, especially if you're less keen on lots of economic models. Graham Hancock's *Lords of Poverty* (Nairobi: Camerapix, 2007) is shrill and unfair, but does expose some real issues.

On the subject of global trade, Joseph Stiglitz and Andrew Charlton's *Fair Trade for All: How Trade Can Promote Development* (Oxford: Oxford University Press, 2005) is an excellent introduction. Collier is also good on this, as is the Commission for Africa report.

The international agencies are a very useful source of information and data. The UK's aid agency DFID is particularly well-regarded for its research output. Papers are available from http://www.dfid.gov.uk/Media-Room/Publications. Reports quoted in the text are 'Communication Matters' (2008), DFID Country Assistance Plan (2009), 'Eliminating World Poverty: Making Globalisation Work for the Poor' (2000) and 'Eliminating World Poverty: Building Our Common Future' (2009). The World Bank is an invaluable source of data, and its reports can be downloaded from http://www.worldbank.org. The World Development Indicators are particularly useful (the 2009 document was quoted here).

I've also referenced a couple of academic papers: Mushtaq Khan, 'The Efficiency Implications of Corruption' in the *Journal of International Development* Vol. 8 No. 5 (1996), pp. 683–696, and Xavier Sala-i-Martin and Maxim Pinkovskiy, 'African Poverty is Falling … Much Faster Than You Think!', which can be found at http://www.columbia.edu/~xs23/papers/pdfs/Africa_Paper_VX3.2.pdf.

Other sources of information are the IMF (http://www.imf.org), the United Nations Development Programme (http://www.undp.org), the Overseas Development Institute (http://www.odi.org.uk) and the World Trade Organisation (http://www.wto.org). Reports quoted from here include the 'Millennium Development Goals Report (UN, 2009), 'Investing in Development: A Practical Plan to Achieve the Millennium Development Goals' (UN, 2005) and 'Aid to Africa: More Doesn't Have to Mean Worse' (ODI, 2005). A fantastic resource for aid and development issues is 'Our Common Interest: Report of the Commission for Africa' (2005) , see http://www.commissionforafrica.info.

## MORAL AND POLITICAL PHILOSOPHY

For an introduction to ancient moral philosophy, the edition of Plato's *Republic* translated by Robin Waterfield (Oxford: Oxford University Press, 1993) is full of invaluable notes and guidance.

Aristotle's *The Nichomachean Ethics*, edited by David Ross (Oxford: Oxford University Press, 1980) is the source of virtue ethics theory, and an excellent companion to that work is Christopher Warne's *Aristotle's Nichomachean Ethics: A Reader's Guide* (London: Continuum, 2006).

For general books on ethics and moral philosophy, Bernard Williams' *Morality: An Introduction to Ethics* (Cambridge: Cambridge University Press, 1972) and *Moral Luck* (Cambridge: Cambridge University Press, 1981) are both extremely thought-provoking, though quite difficult. A very clear exposition of the issues, especially with regard to applied ethics, is Jonathan Glover, *Causing Death and Saving Lives* (Harmondsworth: Penguin, 1977). Peter Singer is one of the most important contemporary philosophers interested in the ethics of aid, and his *The Expanding Circle* (Oxford: Oxford University Press, 1981) is worth reading (see below for papers quoted too). A very useful collection of papers on development ethics is Deen K. Chatterjee (ed.), *The Ethics of Assistance: Morality and the Distant Needy* (Cambridge, Cambridge University Press, 2004).

Some important works of political philosophy quoted are William Godwin, *Enquiry Concerning Political Justice* (Harmondsworth: Penguin, 1976), Jeremy Bentham, *Introduction to the Principles of Morals and Legislation* (Oxford : Clarendon Press, 1996) and John Stuart Mill, *Utilitarianism* (Mineola, NY: Dover, 2007). In addition, Jean Jacques Rousseau's *The Social Contract*, translated by Maurice Cranston (Harmondsworth: Penguin, 1968) is useful both as a source of ideas on equality and for an insight in Rousseau's thoughts on compassion. His *Emile*, translated by Allan Bloom (New York: Basic Books, 1979) has much more on the psychology of pity. Guides to Rousseau are Christopher D. Wraight, *Rousseau's Social Contract* (London: Continuum, 2008) and Nicholas Dent, *Rousseau* (Oxford: Blackwell, 1988).

There's a voluminous literature on John Rawls; political thought. His *The Law of Peoples* (Cambridge, MA: Harvard University Press, 2001) is explicitly concerned with issues of international equality, though the seminal *A Theory of Justice* (Oxford: Oxford

University Press, 1971) is the most important statement of his general approach. For an excellent exposition of the latter, see Jonathan Wolff's *An Introduction to Political* Philosophy (Oxford: Oxford University Press, 1996).

Papers quoted here are Susan Wolf, 'Moral Saints' in *The Journal of Philosophy*, Vol. 79, No. 8 (August 1982), pp. 419–439, John Arthur, 'Famine Relief and the Ideal Moral Code', in *Ethics in Practice* (Oxford: Blackwell, 2007), Peter Singer, 'All Animals are Equal' in *Philosophical Exchange*, Vol. I (1974), Peter Singer, 'Famine, Affluence, and Morality', in Hugh LaFollette (ed.), *Ethics in Practice* (Oxford: Blackwell, 2007) and Thomas Pogge, 'An Egalitarian Law of Peoples' in *Philosophy and Public Affairs*, Vol. 23, No. 3 (1994), pp. 195–224.

## OTHER WORKS REFERRED TO IN THE TEXT

Gregory Clark, *Farewell to Alms: A Brief Economic History of the World* (Princeton: Princeton University Press, 2007).

Joseph Conrad, *Heart of Darkness* (London: Norton & Company, 1971).

Jared Diamond, *Guns, Germs and Steel* (London: Vintage, 1998).

Niall Ferguson, *Empire: How Britain Made the Modern World* (London: Allan Lane, 2003).

Michael Frayn, *A Landing on the Sun* (London: Faber & Faber, 2000).

Matthew Kneale, *English Passengers* (Harmondsworth: Penguin, 2000).

Adam Hochschild, *King Leopold's Ghost* (London: Pan, 2002).

David Livingstone, *Missionary Travels and Researches in South Africa* (1857).

Thomas Malthus, *An Essay on the Principle of Population*, ed. by T. H. Hollingsworth (London: Dent, 1973).

Paul Theroux, *Dark Star Safari: Overland from Cairo to Cape Town* (London: Penguin, 2003).

Anthony Trollope, *Framley Parsonage* (London, The Zodiac Press, 1950).

Max Weber, *The Protestant Ethic and the Spirit of Capitalism*, trans. by Talcott Parsons (London: Routledge, 1992).

C. V. Wedgwood, *The Thirty Years War* (London: The Folio Society, 1999).

David Williams, *Malawi: The Politics of Despair* (London: Cornell University Press, 1978).

## Notes

## Chapter 1

1. Again, at the time of this writing, the scheme looks set to be extended further, possibly for a fourth year.
2. http://www.guardian.co.uk/katine/2007/oct/20/about
3. Katine Community Partnerships Project: Six-Monthly Report, p. 11.
4. 'Reliance on handouts' in the *Guardian* (1 April 2010). Also available at http://www.guardian.co.uk/katine/katine-chronicles-blog/2010/apr/01/reliance-on-handouts
5. I'll use these terms later in the book. They shouldn't be confused with the technical economic sense of 'microeconomic' and 'macro-economic', although there are similar ideas at work.
6. Joseph Conrad, *Heart of Darkness* (London: Norton & Company, 1971), pp. 5–6.
7. When I refer to 'we', I generally mean citizens of Europe and North America, where this book will chiefly be sold. That shouldn't be taken to imply that I think such people are the only, or the most important, voices in the debate over aid and trade. They are, how-ever, generally the ones with the most power to change the way things are done.
8. Description taken from C. V. Wedgwood, *The Thirty Years War* (London: The Folio Society, 1999), pp. 3–4.
9. Max Weber, *The Protestant Ethic and the Spirit of Capitalism*, trans. by Talcott Parsons (London: Routledge, 1992), p. 21.
10. Matthew Kneale, *English Passengers* (Harmondsworth: Penguin, 2000), p. 280. This is a work of fiction, but Kneale makes clear that his

inspiration for the quoted character comes from a real work with similar aims: *The Races of Men: A Fragment* by Robert Knox.

11. Jared Diamond, *Guns, Germs and Steel* (London: Vintage, 1998), p. 405.

12. Diamond, *Guns, Germs and Steel*, p. 172.

13. Drawn from Diamond, *Guns, Germs and Steel*, pp. 406–407.

14. 'Communication Matters' (DFID report, 2008). This attitude is very common in the press. For example, Simon Heffer, writing in the *Daily Telegraph* (18 May 2010), on the policy of the Conservative Government to maintain levels of aid spending inherited from the previous Labour administration: 'They [the electorate] were told their money would continue to be sent to Third World despotisms, further under-mining the economies of those countries, so the Tories could boast that the overseas aid budget was untouched; which is very nice for the wives of those despots on their shopping trips to Paris and Milan, and for the order books of Mercedes-Benz.'

15. See Thomas Malthus, *An Essay on the Principle of Population*, ed. by T. H. Hollingsworth (London: Dent, 1973), pp. 5–11. For a recent dis-cussion of the Malthusian Trap, see Gregory Clark, *Farewell to Alms: A Brief Economic History of the World* (Princeton: Princeton University Press, 2007), p. 20.

16. For more detail on the figures, see Clark, *Farewell to Alms*, pp. 1–3.

17. Clark, *Farewell to Alms*, p. 283.

18. Niall Ferguson, *Empire: How Britain Made the Modern World* (London: Allan Lane, 2003), pp. 358–359.

19. Diamond, *Guns, Germs and Steel*, p. 76.

20. Ferguson, *Empire*, pp. 225–226.

21. Diamond, *Guns, Germs and Steel*, p. 213.

22. Adam Hochschild, *King Leopold's Ghost* (London: Pan, 2002), pp. 165–166.

23. Hochschild, *King Leopold's Ghost*, p. 233.

24. Ferguson, *Empire*, pp.xviii, 368.

25. David Livingstone, *Missionary Travels and Researches in South Africa* (1857).

26. There's an account of this process in colonial-era Malawi in David Williams, *Malawi: The Politics of Despair* (London: Cornell University Press, 1978), p. 87.

27. Jeffrey Sachs, *The End of Poverty: How We Can Make It Happen in Our Lifetime* (London: Penguin, 2005), p. 189.

28. William Eastlerly, *The White Man's Burden: Why the West's Efforts to Aid the Rest Have Done So Much Ill and So Little Good* (Oxford: Oxford University Press, 2006), p. 247.

29. Easterly, *The White Man's Burden*, pp. 247, 249.

30. GDP stands for Gross Domestic Product, and is a common measure of the size of a country's economy. It will be used throughout as an indicator of economic success.

31. Ferguson, *Empire*, p. 360.

32. See, for example, Stephen Krasner of Stanford University, quoted in Easterly, *The White Man's Burden*, p. 238

33. Hochschild, *King Leopold's Ghost*, pp. 301, 302.

34. 'Our Common Interest: Report of the Commission for Africa' (2005), p. 103.

35. 'Our Common Interest', pp. 102, 103.

36. Paul Collier, *The Bottom Billion* (Oxford: Oxford University Press, 2007), p. 3.

## Chapter 2

1. There are some writers who agree with this. See, for example, Garret Hardin, 'Lifeboat Ethics: The Case Against Helping the Poor'. A copy of this can be found at http://www.garrethardinsociety.org/articles/articles.html.

2. David Hume, A Treatise of Human Nature, ed. by L. A. Selby-Bigge (Oxford: Oxford University Press, 1978), p. 469.

3. Plato, Republic, trans. by Robin Waterfield (Oxford: Oxford University Press, 1993), p. 48.

4. See Bernard Williams, Morality: An Introduction to Ethics (Cambridge: Cambridge University Press, 1972), pp. 23–24.

5. Williams, Morality, p. 26.

6. This is a variation on the famous example used by William Godwin in his Enquiry Concerning Political Justice (Harmondsworth: Penguin, 1976).

7.  There's an influential treatment of the psychological aspects of morality, and why bald utilitarian accounts necessarily leave important aspects of it out, in Bernard Williams, Moral Luck (Cambridge: Cambridge University Press, 1981). See especially 'Persons, Character and Reality'.

8.  See, for example, 'All Animals Are Equal' in Philosophical Exchange, I 1974.

9.  Peter Singer, The Expanding Circle (Oxford: Oxford University Press, 1981), p. 109.

10. Singer, The Expanding Circle, p. 120.

11. Singer, 'Famine, Affluence, and Morality', in Hugh LaFollette (ed.), Ethics in Practice (Oxford: Blackwell, 2007), pp. 614, 616.

12. There is a range of papers addressing Singer's thesis in Deen K. Chatterjee (ed.), The Ethics of Assistance: Morality and the Distant Needy (Cambridge, Cambridge University Press, 2004). See especially Singer's own defence in 'Outsiders: Our Obligations to Those Beyond Our Borders' and Richard J. Arneson's 'Moral Limits on the Demands of Beneficence?'.

13. Susan Wolf, 'Moral Saints' in The Journal of Philosophy, Vol. 79, No. 8 (August 1982), p. 421.

14. John Arthur, 'Famine Relief and the Ideal Moral Code', in Ethics in Practice (Oxford: Blackwell, 2007), p. 625.

15. Arthur, 'Famine Relief and the Ideal Moral Code', p. 629.

16. Philippa Foot, 'The Problem of Abortion and the Doctrine of the Double Effect', quoted in Jonathan Glover, Causing Death and Saving Lives (Harmondsworth: Penguin, 1977), p. 93.

17. For a discussion of this, see 'Justifying Physician-Assisted Deaths' in LaFollette (ed.), Ethics in Practice, pp. 72–80.

18. For an account, see 'English rebels who ignored apartheid cause still show a lack of shame', the Guardian, 11 January 2010.

19. Glover, Causing Death and Saving Lives, p. 110.

20. Especially Chapter 7, pp. 92–112.

## Chapter 3

1.  For example, see the article 'Cutting waste at DFID has only just begun' in *The Daily Telegraph* (18 May 2010), which was drawn from

a critical report from the International Policy Network report 'Fake Aid' (April 2010).

2. Jeremy Bentham, *Introduction to the Principles of Morals and Legislation* (Oxford : Clarendon Press, 1996); John Stuart Mill, *Utilitarianism* (Mineola, NY: Dover, 2007).

3. Philosophers' academic jargon is pretty unpleasant, and I try and make as little use of it as possible. I also try and avoid development professionals' jargon, which is also endemic in the academic literature. There are generally very few occasions where normal language is insufficient to explain the concepts being used.

4. Data taken from DFID's 2009 Country Assistance Plan for Malawi (available from http://www.dfid.gov.uk).

5. Michael Frayn, *A Landing on the Sun* (London: Faber & Faber. 2000), p. 84.

6. Taken from the National Institute for Clinical Excellence (NICE) website: http://www.nice.org.uk.

7. For the full text of the UN Universal Declaration of Human Rights, see http://www.un.org/en/documents/udhr/.

8. It should be noted that such approaches are not without their critics, and there are some in the medical community who lament the move away from a more public-health-based strategy. However, the general principle is still worthy of attention here.

9. See Jean Jacques Rousseau, *The Social Contract*, trans. by Maurice Cranston (Harmondsworth: Penguin, 1968), p. 59–62).

10. For more detail on this, see Christopher D. Wraight, *Rousseau's Social Contract* (London: Continuum, 2008), pp. 33–38.

11. John Rawls, *A Theory of Justice* (Oxford: Oxford University Press, 1971), p. 12.

12. Rawls, *A Theory of Justice*, p. 302.

13. Rawls, *A Theory of Justice*, p. 302. Strictly speaking, the Difference Principle is only one half of the second principle of justice, but for reasons of simplicity I've not covered the other provisions.

14. Of course, this is just a sketch. Rawls' complete position is somewhat more complex. He takes into account the possibility that some level of inequality may be tolerated in order to prevent the poorest being less well-off, in an absolute sense, than they otherwise would be,

and there are important qualifications on all the principles of justice. For a more complete statement of his position, see Rawls, *A Theory of Justice*, pp. 302–303.

15. Rawls himself doesn't do this, and his theory is explicitly concerned with the issue of justice within a certain kind of society. We'll touch on this further below.

16. For an extremely clear and helpful discussion of these issues, see Jonathan Wolff, *An Introduction to Political* Philosophy (Oxford: Oxford University Press, 1996), pp. 168–195.

17. See John Rawls, *The Law of Peoples* (Cambridge, MA: Harvard University Press, 2001), pp. 30–35.

18. See, for example, Onora O'Neill, 'Global justice: whose obligations?' in Deen Chatterjee (ed.), *The Ethics of Assistance*, pp. 242–259, and Thomas Pogge, 'An Egalitarian Law of Peoples' in *Philosophy and Public Affairs*, Vol. 23, No. 3 (1994), pp. 195–224.

19. A similar point is made by Roger Scruton in *Philosopher on Dover Beach* (South Bend: St Augustine's Press, 1997), pp. 109–10: 'Utilitarianism represents the attempt by science to take charge of our moral lives: the attempt by the objective perspective to displace the subject from his throne. [. . .] Utilitarianism fails as a moral theory because, aspiring to objectivity, it begins to justify actions in terms which remove the motive to engage in them.'

20. Aristotle, *The Nichomachean Ethics*, ed. by David Ross (Oxford: Oxford University Press, 1980), p. 38 (1106b).

21. In the jargon, virtue ethics is often claimed to be insufficiently *normative* – that is, it doesn't provide a proper guide to action.

22. For a thorough discussion of the issues, see Christopher Warne, *Aristotle's Nichomachean Ethics: A Reader's Guide* (London: Continuum, 2006), especially pp. 13–17.

23. For more details, see Christopher D. Wraight, *Rousseau's Social Contract: A Reader's Guide* (London: Continuum, 2008), pp. 11–18.

24. Rousseau, *Emile*, Book 4, pp. 291–220, quoted in Nicholas Dent, *Rousseau* (Oxford: Blackwell, 1988), pp. 126–127. The sentiment here applies equally well, of course, to women.

25. Rousseau, *Emile*, Book 4, pp. 235, quoted in Dent, *Rousseau*, p.139.

## Chapter 4

1. Anthony Trollope, Framley Parsonage (London, The Zodiac Press, 1950), pp. 27–28.
2. 'Celebrities' Embrace of Africa has Critics', The New York Times, 1 July 2005.
3. UNDP Report of the Administrator, UNDP Budget Estimates for 2010–2011 (2010); World Food Programme fact sheet (September 2009).
4. This is an important distinction, which should be borne in mind in what follows. Activities that aim to eradicate poverty may be very different from those that aim to merely reduce its effects. In fact, it may be that the two aims conflict. It's possible that actions taken to bring about long-lasting prosperity may cause an increase in poverty in the short term. This is one reason the aid agencies often disagree very strongly over each others' methods – their aims are not always as similar as they might appear. We'll see lots of examples of this in the rest of the chapter.
5. Paul Theroux, Dark Star Safari: Overland from Cairo to Cape Town (London: Penguin, 2003), pp. 304, 305; 307.
6. Sachs, The End of Poverty, p. 246.
7. Sachs, The End of Poverty, p. 197.
8. Sachs, The End of Poverty, p. 204.
9. Another example is Korea, which received huge amounts of US aid in the 1950s and 1960s for similar reasons (perhaps as high as £13 billion). Although less well-known, this programme arguably had more similarities with Sachs' approach than did the Marshall Plan.
10. Although he didn't; the quotation refers to the Lend-Lease programme.
11. MDGs taken from Investing in Development: A Practical Plan to Achieve the Millennium Development Goals (UN, 2005).
12. The Millennium Development Goals Report, (UN, 2009).
13. There are other difficulties here. It's not obvious, for example, that the MDGs apply equally well to very different countries (as they're supposed to). Why, for instance, should India have the same goals as Chad – two states with very different economies, histories and

prospects. There has also been criticism over the arbitrariness of the 2012 date. I don't think these criticisms are negligible, but for the sake of simplicity I've not considered them here in detail.

14. It should be noted again here that figures on poverty levels are very hard to derive with any certainty. There are studies that dispute statistics such as these (see, for example, Xavier Sala-i-Martin et al, 'African Poverty is Falling . . . Much Faster Than You Think!', which can be found at http://www.columbia.edu/~xs23/papers/pdfs/Africa_Paper_VX3.2.pdf). However, throughout I have quoted what I take to be mainstream estimates over which there is some degree of consensus.

15. Easterly, The White Man's Burden, pp. 39–40.

16. Easterly, The White Man's Burden, pp. 35–37.

17. Easterly, The White Man's Burden, p. 39.

18. Easterly, The White Man's Burden, pp. 44–45.

19. I'll look at this point in more detail below.

20. Paul Collier, The Bottom Billion (Oxford: Oxford University Press, 2007), p. 66.

21. See his paper 'The Efficiency Implications of Corruption' for a technical account of this. The paper can be downloaded from http://mercury.soas.ac.uk/users/mk17/Docs/articles.htm.

22. An influential Malawian academic once told me he liked Victorian ethics, for precisely that reason.

23. On some measures, participation in civic life is actually higher in Africa than in Europe or America (for example, voter turnout), but it's far from clear that voters actually hold their leaders accountable for malpractice or incompetence in the same way. This is due, it seems to me, to a combination of poor information, poor education, low expectations, and cultural allegiances which are far stronger than ones based on policy choices.

24. Easterly, The White Man's Burden, p. 268.

25. Moreover, legitimate democratic opposition parties can only comment meaningfully on the local government's spending decisions if there's some chance the money could, in principle, be reallocated during the budget process. If aid agencies retain full control over spending decisions, then the domestic political environment is further eroded.

26. For the sake of simplicity, I've presented the debate here as if Sachs and Easterly are the only two choices in an assessment of aid policy. Of course, that's not the case – plenty of aid professionals disagree with both men. However, they do represent two approaches which between them characterize the public debate quite well. Should you wish to delve into the issues more deeply, it's worth remembering that there are almost as many positions on aid and development as there are economists working on the subject.

27. Graham Hancock, Lords of Poverty (Nairobi: Camerapix, 2007), p. 192.

28. Collier, The Bottom Billion, p. 122.

29. Commission for Africa Report, p. 85.

30. 'Celebrities' Embrace of Africa has Critics', The New York Times, 1 July 2005.

31. 'Aid to Africa: More Doesn't Have to Mean Worse', ODI Opinions Paper 43, published in 2005 (available from www.odi.org.uk/publications/opinions).

## Chapter 5

1. 'World Trade Report 2008: Trade in a Globalizing World' (WTO, 2008), p. 15.

2. It's interesting to note that these figures are often used to cast doubt on the effectiveness of aid (as discussed in Chapter 4). If countries like Thailand can escape from poverty through trade, then perhaps international aid is entirely pointless. As ever, the situation is more complex than this. Countries like Korea and Japan achieved their massive leap in productivity partly as a result of government subsidies ('planner' behaviour) and large-scale grants.

3. World Trade Report 2008, p. 139.

4. 'Eliminating World Poverty: Making Globalisation Work for the Poor', White Paper on International Development (Department for International Development, 2000), p. 67.

5. Data taken from World Development Indicators (World Bank, 2009), p. 382. This figure is the total given by the DAC (Development

Assistance Committee) members of the OECD club of rich countries in 2007, and is, by the nature of such things, a vague figure. It excludes aid flows from non-DAC countries, and is reliant on donor countries' reporting mechanisms for individual contributions.

6. World Trade Report 2008, p. 11. This excludes the value of trade in commercial services: another £3 trillion.

7. Robert Calderisi, *The Trouble with Africa* (New Haven: Yale University Press, 2007), p. 144.

8. Collier, *The Bottom Billion*, p. 161.

9. Commission for Africa report, p. 265.

10. Joseph Stiglitz and Andrew Charlton, *Fair Trade for All: How Trade Can Promote Development* (Oxford: Oxford University Press, 2005), p. 189.

11. Commission for Africa report, pp. 296–297; Collier, *The Bottom Billion*, pp. 162–163.

12. Calderisi, *The Trouble with Africa*, p. 143.

13. Commission for Africa report, p. 280.

14. For the Everything But Arms scheme, see the EU website at http://bit.ly/b9SHru. For the AGOA scheme, see http://www.agoa.gov.

15. Commission for Africa report, p. 275.

16. Stiglitz and Charlton, *Fair Trade for All*, pp. 180–183.

17. *Making Globalisation Work for the Poor*, p. 19.

18. *Making Globalisation Work for the Poor*, p. 66.

19. Stiglitz and Charlton, *Fair Trade for All*, p. 47.

20. Stiglitz and Charlton, *Fair Trade for All*, pp. 108–109.

# Index